SPRINGBOARDS FOR DISCUSSION

JOHN H. BRATT

Contemporary Discussion Series

Baker Book House
Grand Rapids, Michigan

ISBN: 0-8010-0510-8

First printing, October 1970
Second printing, March 1971
Third printing, February 1972
Fourth printing, August 1973

Printed in the United States of America

Contents

CUSTOMS AND PRACTICES OF THE EARLY CHURCH

THE END TIME

MORAL PROBLEMS

How about Alcoholism and the Christian? 1

Q. *Can one at the same time be an alcoholic and a Christian?*

A. Alcoholism is viewed in two ways.

Some view it solely as a *moral-spiritual* problem. The drinker has fallen into grievous sin. Drunkenness has become a recurring habit with him. He succeeds one drinking bout with another. Refusing to face the realities of life, he resorts to *escapism*. Life for him is one escape after another. His problem is moral and spiritual. He needs to repent and draw on the help of God. Then only can he successfully cope with his problem.

Others tend to view this mainly as a *health* problem. The alcoholic is disease-infected. He is desperately sick and needs medical and psychiatric attention. He must be treated as a man who is seriously ill.

It would seem that these viewpoints must be conjoined. The alcoholic is indulging in sin, and for this he needs repentance and the saving grace of God. But he is also sick. His illness is self-inflicted, it is true, but he is ill nonetheless. Alcoholism is both a *sin* and a *sickness*.

Caught in the toils of this "sinsickness," can he be a Christian? He can, if two conditions are met. One is that he realizes the seriousness of his plight. The other is that he is determined, with God's help, to solve his problem. If he is genuinely concerned, and if he is drawing on all possible religious, medical, and psychiatric help, the genuineness of his religious commitment should not be impugned.

Once he is "dried out," may the church place temptation in his path by offering him wine in the communion service?

This poses a real moral problem for the consistory of his church.

If the church has any such individual in its membership, it should face the problem squarely. Three possibilities should be considered. It may decide, for the sake of the spiritual welfare of this member of the body of Christ, to use grape juice instead of wine in its communion celebration. It may defend its action by asserting, and rightly so, that the elements have symbolic rather than realistic significance. It may decide to serve him a communion glass of grape juice while the other communicants are served wine. Or it may decide to suggest to him that he partake of communion in one of our churches that serves grape juice to all. At any rate, the church should take cognizance of his problem and seek to resolve it in accord with his spiritual welfare and the concern of the church for all of her members.

Questions

1. What is the Biblical teaching with respect to the legitimacy of strong drink (Ps. 104:15; Prov. 31:6, 7; I Tim. 4:4; 5:23; etc.) and to its abuse (Prov. 20:1; 23:30: Isa. 28:7; Joel 1:5; Eph. 5:18; I Tim. 3:8; etc.)? Can you extract a principle from these passages?

2. Does the fact that our Lord made water into wine at the wedding at Cana, used wine at the institution of the Lord's Supper, and is described by Matthew as "The Son of Man [who] came eating and drinking" have a bearing on the question?

3. Are there weaknesses and dangers in the *drinking in moderation* position?

8

4. It is a known fact that half of the traffic deaths are alcohol related, and that the liquor traffic has become so great that ten times as much is spent for liquor in America as is spent for our educational endeavors. In view of these facts, would it be commendable for the Christian voluntarily to abstain from inbibing all intoxicating beverages as his witness against the present evil?

5. The principle of Christian liberty is frequently appealed to by those who condone drinking. Is this a valid principle to apply? How is the principle qualified? (See Rom. 14:21; I Cor. 6:12, 15, 19; 10:23.)

6. What do you think of the Paterson theory of *circumstantial flexibility*, namely that "a Christian is at liberty to eat or drink anything, except under periodic circumstances that would render the use of his liberty unwise, unedifying, or unloving"?

7. In your estimation. are enough sermons devoted to this problem? Should more light from the Word of God be shed upon it?

8. Is the problem of alcoholism similar to or identical with the drug addiction problem? Is being addicted to marijuana or heroin a worse sin than being an alcoholic?

2 Is It Wrong to Land on the Moon?

Q. *Is the lunar landing an invasion of God's domain?*

A. At the outset it should be established that it was neither sinful nor presumptuous to land on the moon. The universe is vast — it includes not only the earth but the cloudy heaven and the planetary heavens as well — and to explore it and learn more about God's great creation would seem to be within the proper province of man. To be sure, God has given the earth to be the place of habitation for man and He made it to be an elect planet in that He sent His Son to suffer and die on this earth of ours. But that does not say that man may not go outside of it and explore that which lies beyond.

There are, however, at least two dangers implicit in this latest of scientific achievements.

One is a resurgence of *humanism,* a new stress on the "magnificent" abilities of man. The temptation is there to exalt man and assume that there is no limitation to his scientific potential. President Nixon leaned in that direction when he called the period of lunar landing the "greatest week since creation." That is extravagant language. The Bible indicates clearly that the greatest week since creation was either the one in which the Incarnation occurred and Christ was born, or the one in which Christ gave his life on Calvary for the sins of the world. That was God's work; and no human achievement, no matter how impressive it be, can begin to compare with it.

Incidentally there are those today who maintain that we now need a "lunar theology," a "space theology," or an "astrotheology." Not so. The traditional Biblical theology will do. It exalts God in His greatness and majesty as is evident in His words and works. It calls for a sense of humility and awe in the face of His infinite greatness. And that awe and reverence ought to increase as new aspects of the greatness of His universe are unfolded and disclosed.

The second danger of this latest exploit is that of *imbalance* and *distortion of priorities* — when the lure of space exploration and the appeal and glamor of space conquests (along with the ambition to outstrip the other nations) means a neglect of the urgent problems of this planet. A nation, like an individual, must have priorities, and it is very easy in this particular case to throw space exploration all out of proportion to its importance and in so doing eat up too large a share of the national budget. We have some very urgent earthbound problems. Air pollution is becoming a hazard: our rivers and streams are being poisoned and are losing their beauty as well as becoming a health hazard; the ghettos and slums remain a blight on this nation; poverty is widespread in this day of affluence; racism with its prejudice and discrimination needs attacking; and our involvement in Indo-China is a vexing problem. The lunar landing was an example of magnificent team effort, and our nation needs to tackle its domestic and international problems with the same unity and dedication. Proper stewardship of national monies is as imperative as is proper personal stewardship.

Questions

1. Does Psalm 115:16 ("The heavens are the heavens

11

of Jehovah; but the earth hath he given to the children of men") rule out space exploration? Or can we compare space today to America's western frontier two hundred years ago?

2. Should we send up unmanned instead of manned satellites and thus not risk human life in these ventures? Were the deaths of the three astronauts, Grissom, White, and Chaffee, and the near disaster of Apollo 13 warnings from God that such efforts should be discontinued?

3. If an astronaut or astronauts could not re-enter the earth's atmosphere, would he (they) be warranted in taking his (their) own life (lives)?

4. Is the race to the moon and other planets more than a matter of national pride and prestige? If the Soviets had reached the moon first would that have been clear proof of the superiority of the Communistic way of life?

5. It takes atmosphere, water, oxygen, and vegetation to sustain human life. The moon and the planet Mercury have no atmosphere and water; Venus has neither oxygen nor vegetation; and Saturn, Mars, Jupiter, Neptune, and Uranus have vastly wide temperature differentials. Is it not, then, a futile enterprise to seek to land on these planets? Or can you see benefits in addition to providing 400,000 jobs in the space program and thus helping to build up the national economy?

6. The noted scientist, Warren Weaver, maintains that the money spent on space exploration ought to be spent for educational and medical research. He says: "Nothing is more immoral than spending too much money on too few ideas." Do you agree? So long as there are Americans living beneath the subsistence level and starvation occurs in many parts of the world, is spending for space exploration good stewardship of our monies?

Is Capital
Punishment Biblical? 3

Q. *Is there basis in Scripture for capital punishment?*

A. Those who argue for its abolition maintain that capital punishment is unfair, since anyone with money and legal means can establish "temporary insanity; capital punishment is tremendously expensive, since it involves an almost unending chain of appeals; it does not deter murder; it presupposes infallible judicial procedure; and it is unbiblical.

If you insist that Genesis 9:6 ought to be taken literally, so they say, then the death penalty ought to be levied, too, for adulterers (Lev. 20:10) and those who maltreat their fathers or mothers (Exod. 21:15). Consistency would demand this. When Jesus dealt with the woman guilty of a capital offense (John 8:1-11) He did not demand the death penalty. It is true that Romans 13 refers to the "sword," but that is simply a symbol of judicial authority, since the Romans did not literally execute by means of the sword.

They further maintain that the New Testament nowhere demands it, in fact, it warns against anything that appears retaliatory or as paying back in like coin, and stresses instead the law of love (see Sermon on the Mount).

Those who argue in favor of capital punishment maintain that the Old Testament speaks directly to the civil order (our social and political life) and demands this form of punishment. Exodus 20:13 ("Thou shalt not kill") has no bearing on the question, since it deals only with murder itself. John 8 may not be in the original text of the Scriptures and, even if it is, it does not concern itself with this question. It simply teaches — so they argue — Jesus' right and authority to forgive sin. It is true that in Matthew 5:17 Jesus speaks about fulfilling the law, but He does not mean thereby "to destroy the basic principles of law and order, righteousness and justice." Furthermore, Romans 13 means just what is says: the government does have the right in some instances to take human life.

This problem has to do with the relationship of the Old Testament to the New Testament. And that is no easy question. We know that the New Testament does modify the Old Testament, but also that the moral law of the Old Testament is always binding. Perhaps a thorough study of this question will lead to some firm conclusions.

Questions

1. It is sometimes said that capital punishment is barbaric, a throwback to the days of primitive vengeance, that it is possible to execute an innocent man, and that it cuts off any further hope of repentance on the part of the condemned. What do you think of these arguments against capital punishment?

2. In the Middle Ages, heresy or false teaching was punishable by death on the basis of Exodus 22:20. We no longer regard that as legitimate since our understanding of the Scriptures has progressed. Is it not possible that the same will be true of capital punishment?

3. Pastor John Robinson, in bidding the Pilgrims farewell in 1619, said to them: "God has yet more light to flash forth from His Word." Are we receptive to new interpretations of the Bible? Or are we suspicious of them? How can we tell if they are advancements or perversions?

14

4. Aquinas, the medieval theologian, wrote: "Heresy is a sin ... for which the heretic deserves not only to be put out of the society of the faithful by excommunication but also out of the society of men by death." The true doctrine was regarded as so serious as to demand the death penalty for its denial. Have we swung to the other extreme today when sincerity is the test of a person's beliefs?

5. Abraham Kuyper said of Romans 13:4 ("he [the magistrate] beareth not the sword in vain for he is a minister of God, an avenger of wrath to him that doeth evil") that it implies the power of the *sword of order,* the state may quell rebellion and insure law and order; the *sword of war,* the state may defend itself against attack; and the *sword of justice,* the state may punish the criminal. Do you agree? Does the *sword of justice* imply the right of capital punishment?

6. Should our court procedures be speeded up so that murder trials are not so costly?

7. Does Genesis 2:7 and 3:3, 22 teach such sanctity of human life that no one, not even the state, may violate it?

8. The Old Testament distinguishes between sins done in ignorance (Num. 35:11-23) and sins done deliberately (Num. 35:27-31). Does this have any bearing on the question of capital punishment? Are sins committed in ignorance excusable?

9. In Old Testament times, was the death penalty carried out for those who were guilty of gross sins (murder, blasphemy, etc.) but who repented? Or did a sin or trespass offering take care of the offense? (See Leviticus laws.) David was guilty of both adultery and murder in the Uriah-Bathsheba episode. He repented (Ps. 32; 51) and his life was spared. What is the significance of this account?

10. The opposite of capital punishment is *life prolongation.* Physicians are committed to keeping a person alive as long as possible even if it means extension of misery. Is this in keeping with the Scriptures? Or are "mercy killings" (e.g. withholding drugs and medicines, etc.) permissible?

4 May a Christian Be a Conscientious Objector?

Q. *May a Christian declare himself a pacifist or a conscientious objector?*

A. Almost everyone condemns militarism, the attitude of mind that glorifies war as an instrument of national policy. Fewer condemn pacifism, the position that assumes that since sin is at the root of war (and this is true) all wars therefore are sinful and a Christian has no business participating in them. Pacifism, however, is based on a misuse of some Biblical passages (for example, Matthew 5:38, 39) and involves refusal to support our government. Wars are inevitable in a sinful world, and it is the Christian's duty to support the civil government's call to arms.

But what about the Christian conscience? Must the conscience in all cases yield to governmental command?

The answer is No.

When the government levies a command that runs counter to the command of God — for instance, forbidding the proclamation of the gospel — the Christian is duty bound to refuse obedience in accordance with the declaration of Peter that "we must obey God rather than men" (Acts 5:29).

But what about the circumstance of a particular war and its application to the individual conscience? What, for instance, would the war in Vietnam have to do with the conscience of a Christian who is called to the colors?

There are those who, on grounds of conscience, refuse to take part in any war when, and as long as, they are not persuaded of the justice of a given war. But, as God demands, the rights of conscience must yield priority to the duty of obedience to the government. Uncertainty as to the justice of a given war can be no justifiable ground for refusing obedience to the government.

There is, however, a qualification. If the Christian has made a thorough appraisal of the situation (and this is obviously very difficult, since no one knows whether he has all of the facts at his disposal), is able to marshall intelligent and strong grounds, and is *absolutely certain* in his own mind, in obedience to the light of the Word of God, that his country is fighting for a wrong cause, he may adopt the conscientious objector position and offer his services to the medical or social service corps.

The problem is not a simple one. In a real sense God is the only lord of the conscience, since everyone is responsible to God for all his actions. But that conscience too has been infected by sin. Paul confesses that his persecution of the Christian church had the approbation of his conscience prior to his conversion. He writes in his autobiography, "I verily thought with myself, that I ought to do many things contrary to the name of Jesus of Nazareth" (Acts 26:9). His conscience too needed conversion, and submission of the conscience to God comes in the way of submission to the Word of God which informs and enlightens it. Paul also insists that conscience must yield to the civil government (Rom. 13:1, 5). But that too has its limitations, for when the latter contravenes the Word of God, the Christian is duty bound to repudiate the government and give his highest loyalty to God.

QUESTIONS

1. Prior to July 15, 1970, conscientious objection to war

was recognized only if based on "religious training and belief." On that date, however, the Supreme Court ruled that one need no longer claim religious conviction but his convictions must be respected "if he has strong moral or ethical objections to war in any form." He must have "deeply and sincerely held beliefs which impose upon him the duty of conscience to refrain from participating in any war." It is possible for a draft board to rule on one of these cases? Do you think that religious beliefs should be the only basis?

2. Is it justifiable for one to seek conscientious objector status if one is not convinced or persuaded that a given war is just? Is uncertainty a proper ground?

3. What do you think of the common slogan: "Let your conscience be your guide?"

4. St. Augustine in the early church called *just wars*: "Those which avenge injuries or repel aggression and those which are fought with Christian love against the enemy." Thomas Aquinas in the Middle Ages said that in order for a war to be just it "must be fought with a reasonable possibility of victory, must discriminate between soldiers and civilians, and there must be proportionality between the amount of harm done by the war and the benefits that are anticipated." In more recent times Ryan and Boland claim that a just war "must have been declared by a legitimate authority, must have a just and grave cause, proportionate to the evils it brings about, must be undertaken only after all means of peaceful solution have been attempted without success, must have a serious chance of success, and must be carried out with the right intentions." What do yo think of these criteria?

5. War always brings with it unspeakable inhumanities and brutalities like the My Song massacre in the Vietnam War. In our atomic age, it also carries with it the possibility of wiping out huge areas of civilization. Would these facts be adequate bases on which to register conscientious objection? Has war with its modern weapons of destruction reached such a stage that it can only be immoral and unjustifiable?

How about Cremation? 5

Q. *Is cremation compatible with the Christian faith?*

A. There is no specific command in the Bible to the effect that burial is the only proper way to dispose of a dead body nor is there a specific prohibition of cremation, the burning of the corpse, placing the ashes in an urn, or scattering them to the four winds.

The whole tenor of Scripture, however, and the attitude of the Christian church throughout the centuries is acceptance of the former and looking askance at or condemnation of the latter.

Cremation has been defended on the grounds that the manner of disposal of the body is really of minor importance since the redeemed soul will be housed in a new body; that it is more in keeping with the dignity of the present body that it be reduced to ashes rather than undergo a process of decay and decomposition by the rotting of tissue and the invasion of worms; that it is more sanitary and hygienic; that it involves considerably less expense; that in heavily congested parts of the world, where every foot of ground is precious, it provides one solution to the problem of space; and that the Bible does not expressly forbid it and therefore classes it with the adiaphora or indifferent things.

Contrary to this view, however, it can be argued that the Bible gives strong support to burial as the proper method of disposition of the dead body. It does this negatively by specifying burning of the corpse as a punishment for sin. Incest and harlotry were to be punished in this way in ancient Israel (Lev. 20:14; 21:9). And when Achan had violated the terms of the capture of Jericho by taking as booty some gold and silver and a Babylonian garment, he was condemned to death by stoning and burning (osh. 7:15). Through the prophet Amos, God informed Israel that His judgment is to come upon neighboring Moab and one of the reasons for it is that the Moabites had committed the crime of burning the bones of the king of Edom into lime (Amos 2:1-2).

With respect to the method of burial it must be borne in mind that one of the penalties attached to sin from the very beginning was a "return to the ground" (Gen. 3:19) and a reidentification with the dust of the earth from which man had been originally made. That terminology certainly looks in the direction of burial and so the Old Testament saints construed it. It was predicted to Abraham that he would be buried having achieved a ripe old age (Gen. 15:15). God Himself buried Moses on Mt. Nebo (Deut. 34:6). And how frequently the words "he died and was buried" occur in the summary of the lives of the Old Testament people (Gen. 35:8; 35:19; Num. 20:1; Deut. 10:6; Judg. 8:32, etc.).

There are two Old Testament passages that cremationists appeal to in support of their position. One of them is I Samuel 31:12 where it is recorded that the valiant men of Jabesh-Gilead recovered the bodies of Saul and his sons after their disastrous defeat in battle, carried them back to Jabesh, and burnt them there. The second passage is II Chronicles 16:14 where the Bible speaks of a "very great burning" at the burial of King Asa. With regard to the first passage it must be remembered that Jabesh-Gilead was an Ammonite (pagan, that is) city captured by Saul and the inhabitants were very likely still saddled by some of their heathenish customs, and in the second passage a careful reading of the text will show that Asa himself was buried and the funeral spices were burned on that occasion.

The New Testament church faced the question too of the proper disposal of the body after death had occurred. Theirs was a two-fold choice. Both cremation and burial was practiced by the Greeks, Romans, Babylonians, and Egyptians. The Christian church elected to follow the Jewish method of burial.

They did so merely because they were following, in the main, the Jewish tradition. They did so because there were intimations to that end in the words of their Lord. He said, for instance, about the great resurrection day, "The hour cometh in which all that are in the tombs shall hear his voice and shall come forth; they that have done good, unto the resurrection of life; and they that have done evil, unto the resurrection of judgment" (John 5:28-29). He also spoke of death in terms of sleep from which one would eventually awake. That symbolism is foreign to cremationism. Cremation speaks of total extinction of being.

There was also the example of the Lord. After his atoning death, He was buried in a tomb hewn out of rock. A grave or tomb therefore, and not a crematorium, was sanctified by the Lord. In this regard too the Christian desires to emulate his Lord. Furthermore, the Pauline teachings lean in that direction. In I Corinthians 15, the famous resurrection chapter, the body that is reabsorbed into the earth is analagous to a seed planted in the soil and the newly fashioned glorified body (which is identical with and yet different from the present body) is likened to the harvest. So too the comparison of burial with baptism in Romans 6:3-7 and Colossians 2:12 loses its essential meaning if the former is not literally intended. And Paul terms the body a "temple of God" (I Cor. 3:16-17). He warns in these words, "If any man destroyeth the temple of God, him shall God destroy; for the temple of God is holy and such are ye."

The early church fathers were strong proponents of burial as the only proper method of disposition. Tertullian called cremation a symbol of hell and Cyprian regarded the act as the equivalent of apostasy. Lactantius expressed their commonly accepted views when he said, "We will return the image and workmanship of God to the earth, from which it had its origin."

In the Bible itself and from it in the confessions and liturgies of the Christian church emerges a strong presumption in favor of burial as the proper mode of disposal of the dead.

QUESTIONS

1. What do you think of the following explanation of the position of the Jews on burial and cremation? "In Semitic thought [the Jews were Semites], since the unity of the personality was strongly stressed, the soul was so identified with the body that an annihilation of the body was thought to be virtually synonymous with the destruction of the soul."

2. In I Samuel 31:11-12 we read that when the men of Jabesh-Gilead heard that the Philistines had decapitated Saul and fastened his body to the wall at Bethshan, they remembered Saul's kindnesses to them in previous days, took down his body from the wall, burnt it at Jabesh and buried the ashes. How do you account for this method of disposition?

3. Would you say that the decay or decomposition of the body is part of the penalty for sin and cremation is an effort to sidestep that penalty?

4. Monica, the mother of Augustine, died far from her

native land. On her deathbed she asked to be buried where she died since, she said, "God will be able to find me on the Great Resurrection." Did she mean to imply that the method of disposal of the body was immaterial and unimportant, except for personal sentiment?

5. If the time comes that, because of population expansion, there is no available acreage for a burial ground, would cremation be justifiable?

6. Occasionally at funerals Christians seem to attach too much importance to the body of their loved one and have difficulty detaching themselves from it. Would that heathenish element be eliminated if cremation were in vogue?

7. Jehovah's Witnesses believe in the annihilation of the souls of the wicked. Would cremation harmonize with such a theology?

6 Is There a Case for Gambling?

Q. *Is gambling wrong?*

A. Let us examine some of the arguments "In Defense of Gambling."

Some contend that gambling is merely "entertainment," "healthy fun" that relieves "the dullness of life." But gambling cannot be reduced to those simple terms. It is far from being an innocent form of entertainment. In fact, the criminal element in our society feeds on it. As L. M. Starkey pointed out in a recent issue of the *Christian Century,* "Public gambling provides the treasure chest of the underworld." This so-called innocent form of entertainment has taken on ominous proportions. As the late Attorney General Robert F. Kennedy stated in the *Atlantic,* "What we do know is that the American people are spending more on gambling than on medical care or education; that, in so doing, they are putting up the money for the corruption of public officials and the vicious activities of dope peddlers, loan sharks, and so forth.... Corruption and racketeering, financed largely by gambling, are weakening the vitality and strength of the nation."

A second argument advanced is that gambling is instinctive in human nature and that, since it is natural to man, it ought to be controlled, not eliminated. But not so. Gambling is an expression of man's evil nature. One might as well say that the urge to adultery is natural with man and hence should not be condemned. Gambling is a vice that is developed and promoted. As the Massachusetts Crime Commission which investigated legalized pari-mutuel betting in that state reported, "Gambling is an acquired habit, and nothing shows this more clearly than the manner in which it was stimulated and grew under the opening wedge of the pari-mutuel system."

A third argument advanced is that this is an excellent source of revenue for the state. Here is a good way to stay solvent. But that is an argument of expediency. The state has an ethical as well as an economic responsibility. The Chief of Police of Los Angeles wrote, "Any society that bases its financial structure upon the weaknesses of its people does not deserve to survive." And, for a church that has a spiritual as well as a moral responsibility, to promote gambling to take care of its charities is most reprehensible.

The Archbishop of Canterbury may say that he has no religious objections to gambling, and the Roman Catholic church may condone it — this 50-billion-dollar-a-year vice — but the fact is that it runs counter to a body of Biblical teaching.

The Bible teaches that man is a steward of himself, his money, and his possessions. He must handle his finances responsibly, acting as a trustee of them under God. This means that he may not squander them nor recklessly risk them to the turn of the wheel or the drawing of a card.

The Bible teaches that man must love his neighbor and promote his interest. How can he do this if he seeks to win at the expense of another's losing? To gamble is to be covetous, and covetousness is sternly condemned (I Tim. 6:10, Eph. 5:5, etc.).

The Bible stresses industry, thrift, and diligence. One passage among many, Proverbs 22:29 states, "Seest thou a man diligent in his business? he shall stand before kings; he shall not stand before mean men." Our possessions are to be acquired only by work except for gifts others give us. A gambler is essentially an idler with a "something for nothing" philosophy. And idleness, too, finds stern and repeated condemnation in the Word of God (Prov. 6:6; 10:4, 5; 19:15; 22:13; 24:30, 31; 26:16; I Tim. 5:13, and so forth).

No Christian should stoop to this practice.

QUESTIONS

1. Christians must be on the alert for opportunities to witness. Too often it is difficult to tell the difference between a Christian and a non-Christian. Should we use the opportunity to show our colors by refusing to enter a raffle at the plant, for instance? Should differences between Christians and non-Christians be far more perceptible than they are today? Were the differences more obvious in the early church?

2. What do you think of the argument that since people will bet and gamble anyway (at racetracks, ball games, etc.) we may as well collect taxes on their gambling and use the moneys for a good cause since otherwise the money will go to the underworld?

3. How strict should one be in respect to gambling? Should betting a small sum of money to lend interest to a game of cards be construed as gambling? How about a nickel a hole in a game of golf?

4. Is the purchase of stock on the stock market a form of gambling? Or is there a difference between buying stocks at random and investing after careful investigation?

5. Occasionally we hear the statement, "Life is a gamble." Is there some truth in this observation?

6. Gambling is based on the "chance" factor in life. How do you understand these "chance" passages in the Bible: Deuteronomy 22:6; I Samuel 6:9; II Samuel 20:1; Ecclesiastes 9:11; and Luke 10:31?

7. Some religious groups frown on card playing as a game of chance, contending that it is playing with the providence of God. How valid is this criticism? Can anyone toy with the providence of God?

7 Can a Homosexual Be Saved?

Q. *Can a homosexual be saved?*

A. Homosexuality, traced by Paul in Romans 1 to progressive declension from God, is severely denounced in the Bible. Sodom and Gomorrah were destroyed in large part because of this vile sin, and Paul is unequivocal in I Corinthians 6:9 when he lists it with other grievous sins, unconfessed and unforgiven, that bar from the kingdom of God.

In the face of these stern denunciations, modern attempts to whitewash the vice are reprehensible. Some time ago a number of homosexuals held a Homophile Convention in Washington, D.C. It was a brazen attempt to make a despicable vice respectable. Isaiah's judgment is relevant: "Woe to them that call evil good" (5:20).

But is not homosexuality a sickness? It is a sickness only in the sense that it is self-induced. That is, it constitutes a vice that is pampered and in so doing it locks the victim in its foul clutches. But it is not a sickness like malaria or scarlet fever. Those sicknesses come despite precautions that are taken, and rest in the providence of God. They demand neither confession nor forgiveness. Homosexuality is a vice, the fruitage of violation of the laws of God.

Some take a dim view of the curability of homosexuality. Not so the apostle Paul. He was acquainted with it in his day. The vice was rampant in the Roman empire. And the church at Corinth had been infected with it. But these former homosexuals had been cured. Says the apostle: "And such were some of you: but ye were washed, but ye were sanctified, but ye were justified in the name of the Lord Jesus Christ, and in the Spirit of our God" (I Cor. 6:11). They had undoubtedly made a clean break with the vice. (There is no more possibility for a homosexual to be cured by cutting down on the frequency than for an alcoholic to be cured by tapering off his drinks.)

For one who uses all the helps that are provided, is sincere in his resolution for the new life, and makes a clean break, there is forgiveness in God's grace. Homosexuality is not the unpardonable sin. God promises the power of His Spirit, and for the truly penitent who shows genuineness by absolute abstention, this sin is stricken from the record.

QUESTIONS

1. What does the Bible teach about sodomy, defilement of man with man, in such passages as Leviticus 20:13; Deuteronomy 23:17; I Kings 14:24; 15:12; 22:46; II Kings 23:7; and Job 36:14?

2. Among the pagan nations of Greece and Rome, homosexuality, called pederasty, was very common. The early church regarded it as a monster offense and exacted heavy penalties for it. Such Christian emperors as Constantius and Theodosius also legislated strongly against it, the former decreeing death by the sword for it and the latter, burning the offender alive. Were these penalties too severe?

3. Sexual deviates now have an interdenominational church in Los Angeles, pastored by a self-acknowledged homosexual. Is this a healthy development?

4. What can and should the church do to help the homosexual?

5. Is homosexuality due to heredity or environment?

What can parents do to avoid this development in the sons of the family?

6. What are the dangers in placing vices in the category of sickness?

7. There are those who say that "Sex is a beautiful and sacred thing" while others say that "Man's sexual nature is his lower nature." On the basis of such passages as Genesis 1:27; 2:23-25, etc. who is right?

8. This is called the *enlightened age* as far as sex is concerned. Does that mean an advancement or retrogression? Should we have sex education in our schools?

9. What can the church do to counteract portrayals of sex perversion so common in current novels, plays, and movies?

May Hypnotism Be Used as a Plaything? 8

Q. *May hypnotism be used for purposes of entertainment?*

A. Hypnotism has been defined as "a particular form of direct suggestion" and as "exaggerated suggestibility." Hypnosis is a trance-like condition in which the patient appears to lose the ability to act volitionally and become subject to the will of the hypnotist.

The science of hypnotism is relatively new. Dr. A. A. Liebault (1823-1904) is acknowledged as the "father of modern hypnotism." He coaxed one of his patients to relax and doze off, and then administered a dose of curative suggestions. Earlier, Franz Mesmer (1734-1815), a Viennese physician discovered animal magnetism; Marquis de Puyseque discovered hypnotic somnambulism in 1784; and Dr. Braid developed the science and coined the term *hypnotism* in the 1840's.

The most common technique employed is to induce something that resembles sleep. (The word *hypnotism* is derived from a Greek word meaning *sleep*.) He is asked to seat himself and fix his gaze on a specific point, usually a shiny object, while the operator monotonously intones something suggesting relaxation and drowsiness. The subject's eyelids droop, flutter, and close; and he is apparently in a trance. He is then presented with some challenge (to open his eyes, bend his arm, or something similar). If he obeys the order, the hypnotism has been unsuccessful. If he is powerless to do so, he is in the hypnotic state. The operator may further test him by a pinprick. If he is immune to it, he has fallen into the state of anesthesia that accompanies hypnotism. Now the operator speaks to him by way of urgent suggestion, and the subject obeys. He may recall events of the far distant past and he may perform muscular feats that are impossible for him in normal life. Apparently he has relinquished his moral self-management, has no will of his own, and obediently follows the dictates of the operator.

Some constructive uses are claimed for hypnotism. Psychiatrists have used it in treatment for mental troubles, for instance, the malady of hysteria. Dentists have extolled the use of it to control saliva flow, and to prevent gagging and capillary bleeding. Criminologists claim that it may be useful in detecting crime. And physicians have used it quite extensively. Many shy away from its use because they fear that their patients regard it as a form of quackery.

The American Medical Association legitimatized the use of hypnotism in 1958. It has been used to relieve headaches, set fractures, and clear up skin disorders. It has been helpful as a sort of sedative or tranquilizer to allay anxiety. It has been employed with some success in diseases that have a strong psychosomatic (influence of mind on body) component, for instance, an ulcerous condition. And it has been found to be especially helpful as an adjunct to surgery, that is in the control and elimination of pain. Some maintain however that the patient does suffer while in the hypnotic trance although he cannot remember it upon awaking. It has certainly impelled the medics to view their patients not merely as physical entities but as whole persons, those whose minds and nervous systems have a real bearing on the physical. As Hippocrates, the father of medicine, once put it: "It is more important to know what kind of person has a disease than to know what kind of disease a person has."

Reputable medical men claim that there are many danger areas connected with hypnotism. G. N. Estabrooks (author of *Hypnotism,* E. P. Dutton and Co., New York) lists several of them: undesirable personality changes ("It may leave him so suggestible that he is at the mercy of everyone who, for whim or experiment, may choose to throw him into a trance"); the development of psychoses (diseases or disorders of the mind); placing a person in a position where he may be induced to do criminal or unsocial acts; and the ill effects that follow if one is not thoroughly aroused out of the trance. It is highly questionable whether (except for medical reasons) one may relinquish his own personality in this way and place it under the control of another. We always need to act as morally responsible creatures of God.

Questions

1. Read the witch of Endor episode in I Samuel 28. Is it possible that on this occasion the witch exercised hyponotism over Saul?

2. In hypnotism the experimenter is responsible for the actions of the one whom he hypnotizes. Do we have a right as Christians to yield our wills to others in this way? Suppose that the hypnotist would tell his patient to engage in an immoral act or place his life in jeopardy. May a person delegate his moral responsibility in this way?

3. Some Bible scholars claim that Christ's miracles show the sovereignty of the mind over matter. It is said, for instance, that some supposed cases of leprosy in the New Testament were actually cases of dermatitis caused by nervous tension and that when Jesus allayed the tensions the malady was cured. Comment on this theory.

4. What does the Bible say about the relationship of mind and body? (See Rom. 7:25; 8:7; Eph. 2:3; Col.

2:18.) What does it mean to love God with the mind (Matt. 22:37)?

5. Reflect on this statement by Estabrooks: "Hypnotism may explain many forms of insanity."

Does Christianity Support Pacifism? 9

Q. *Since Christ never took up arms against His enemies, is it not true that Christianity must support pacifism?*

A. It is true that Christ never carried nor used any weapon of war.

He did not, however, hesitate to use force on occasion. When the commercialists invaded the temple precincts, He took a whip of cords and lashed away at them until they beat a hasty retreat. He thereby indicated that the time does come when words no longer suffice and one must resort to the use of force.

And since that day the Christian church, using Saint Paul's teaching that the government holds authority from God and is authorized to use the sword (Rom. 13:1, 4), has held that governments are empowered and duty bound, if the occasion demands it, to use armed force to deter the lawless, preserve liberty, and enforce justice and righteousness in human relations.

It is clear from the Bible that militarism or glorification of war is certainly to be condemned. War is a great evil and it may not be idealized. In the '30's, the German Nazis exalted war. Our Lord intimated clearly that a war-mongering nation is simply sowing the seeds of its own destruction when he said, "All they that take the sword shall perish with the sword" (Matt. 26:52). It is true that He also said, "I came not to send peace, but a sword" (Matt. 10:34), but then He was

35

speaking figuratively. In the context of conversion He predicted that friends and family groups would be broken up when some of them accepted His salvation and others stubbornly refused it.

But how about pacifism, the belief that all war is sinful and wrong? Scripture is often misused in support of the pacifistic position. Its supporters have used such arguments as these: the sixth commandment forbids all killing; Christ is love personified and is called the Prince of Peace; and the Lord taught that if someone strikes us on the one cheek, we are to turn to him the other. The sixth commandment does forbid murder and the emotion of hate that nurtures murder, but that is directed to the individual.

As Genesis 9:6 and Romans 13:4 teach, the state is entrusted with the right of capital punishment and the use of the sword in the exercise of justice and righteousness. (The Christian defense of the war in Vietnam follows that line of thought. Our government is attempting to preserve the freedom of the Vietnamese and is seeking to prevent the Communists from perpetrating acts of injustice and unrighteousness upon a weaker nation.)

It is true that Christ is love personified, but He is also the epitome of justice. Some of His strongest denunciations are directed against oppression and injustice in His day, and He himself gave His life to satisfy the justice of God. He is called in the Scriptures the Prince of Peace, but that must be interpreted spiritually, as far as human history is concerned. He restores peace between an offended God and offending man. It is true that ultimate political peace will come throught Him, but that will be at the end of history when He comes again on the clouds in glory.

And it is true that Jesus stressed the quality of meekness and willingness to suffer at the hands of another when He talked in terms of turning the other cheek, but then He was speaking in the context of private ethics. He was referring to the attitude the individual Christian should take when in his dealings with others he is unjustly provoked or reproached.

The historic position of the Christian church, with appeal to the Scriptures, has been a validation of just war and a condemnation of pacifism.

Questions

1. How is war viewed in the Old Testament? (See Deut. 20; Joshua 1; Ps. 2:2; Eccl. 3:18, etc.) and in the New Testament? (Mark 13:7; James 4:1-2).

2. Is is possible that the command to invade Canaan is the only *Holy War* authorized in the Bible? What do you think of the command to exterminate all of the Canaanites (Deut. 20:16-17)? Can this be morally justified?

3. If the rules laid down in Exodus 20:13; Matthew 5:39, 44; John 13:34; and Romans 12:20 apply to individual relationships, why shouldn't they also apply to nations?

4. When the Bible speaks of war it does so in terms of conventional weapons since it long antedates the Atomic Age. Now, with nuclear weapons, we have unlimited capacity for destruction and in their use in war, the attendant evils would far outweigh the possible benefits. Does this look in the direction of a Pacifistic approach?

5. In Micah 4:3 there is the prediction of a warless world. To what does this refer? this age? the millennium? the eternal world?

6. What do you think of the following judgment: "Violence in the form of war is permissible only in cases of defense of self, family, and country?"

7. Give your estimate of the new view of violence: "Striking a man is violence, but hitting a man's personality is also violence. When we do and say things which weaken

or destroy another's faith in himself or in his God, we do him violence."

8. What can Christian parents do to counteract the pervasive violence in our society as it comes to expression in movies, television and the paperbacks of our day?

9. Ask one of your members to research the Quakers, especially with a view to the basis of their pacifistic views. Analyze their objections to war and military service. How can President Nixon, as a devout Quaker, continue the IndoChina war?

Is Population Control Acceptable? 10

Q. *Is population control acceptable?*

A. The population explosion is one of the problem areas of our time.

A few statistics may highlight the problem.

At the time of Christ the world population was 250,000,000. By 1700 it had doubled, though the increase had been kept down by pestilence, famine, and war. But between 1700 and 1850 it doubled once again. In the next century, due to a massive health program and antibiotics, it tripled and reached 3 billion. And now it is estimated that by the year 2000, if the Lord tarries, it will reach 7 billion.

One of the solutions proposed is large-scale distribution of birth control information and devices.

Back in the eighteenth century, an economist, Malthus by name, noted that population tended to increase much more rapidly than food production and advocated some form of birth control. In America, in this century, the pioneer of birth control was a registered nurse, Margaret Sanger, who was appalled at the high infant mortality and the lack of proper care for children in low-income homes. She opened up a birth control clinic in 1916, was arrested as a "public nuisance," but later was released and was able to secure permission to send this kind of information through the mails.

Now the question is coming to the fore because· of

rapid population gains — especially in such economically underdeveloped countries as China, India, Africa, Pakistan, and Latin America.

What is the Christian approach to this problem? Shall we rely on the providence of God to offer the solution? We certainly must. But God works through responsible creatures. And what is our responsibility in this area? Do the words of Genesis 1:28 "Let them have dominion," have a bearing on it?

There is no doubt in my mind that there are *priorities* of action.

One of them is top-level production of food and maximum use of the riches of the soil. The earth has tremendous natural resources. The United Nations development committee estimates that we could easily increase production of food by 20 percent. We are stewards of the resources God has given, and to plough under crops, pour milk down the drain, and curtail production to keep a balanced economy is unconscionable in my estimation.

A second is the urgent need to curtail waste of food. America is notorious in this regard. The Scriptural example of taking up the baskets of fragments after food distribution lays the emphasis here.

Another priority is aid by wealthy and affluent nations to the underprivileged ones. The Biblical word is that we are our "brother's keepers" and "to whom much is given [physically as well as spiritually] of him much is also required." Shipments of drugs, foodstuffs, and medical supplies as well as technological tips, better methods of agriculture, increased industrialization, and so on, is mandatory.

But suppose that all of these priorities are met, and the problem still remains; then is birth control the solution? The November 8, 1968, issue of the commendable evangelical periodical *Christianity Today* is devoted to this question. The writers take the affirmative position in the main, arguing on Scriptural grounds that love for others and concern for the welfare of others implies refusal to bring into the world children who cannot be adequately cared for.

Two things are quite certain. One is that the priorities must first be conscientiously attempted, and the other is that birth control may never be a matter of governmental mandate. The ultimate decision must always rest on conscience. In Christian terms, this is a personal matter between the marriage partners and God.

Questions

1. Since the purpose of marriage is not only the begetting of children but the loving, lifelong companionship of husband and wife (Gen. 2:18ff) is not birth control legitimate?

2. Is Psalm 127:3, 5 ("Lo, children are an heritage of Jehovah and the fruit of the womb is His reward. . . . Happy is the man who has his quiver full of them") a Biblical prescription for a large family? Or did this apply only to the Old Testament?

3. Is the record of the sin of Onan in Genesis 38:9 a virtual condemnation of birth control? Or is it designed to show lack of respect for the Levirate law (Deut. 25:5-10)?

4. Does Paul advocate celebacy as a general rule in I Corinthians 7? Or is it simply his personal opinion (vss. 6, 12, 25)? Does he recommend it only to those who have the gift (vs. 7)? Or does it apply only in the emergency (vs. 29)?

5. If the government should refuse to grant income tax allowances to more than two children in a family, should the Christian object on moral and spiritual grounds?

6. On July 1, 1970, in line with the pressure for the liberalization of abortion laws, New York passed a law "requiring only that the operation be performed by a licensed physician in a certified medical facility." This was in line

with the thinking of the president of Planned Parenthood who advocated that "abortion be placed in the same category as other health services, a decision between the doctor and his patient." Is this acceptable to the Christian?

7. Does a new human being begin at conception, thus making abortion murder? In the case of a spontaneous miscarriage, is the life of a human being extinguished?

8. Karl Barth mentions the case of Roman Catholic nuns who were raped when the Russians invaded Germany in 1945. These nuns were not allowed by the church to free themselves from the consequences by resorting to abortion. Some Protestant theologians adopted the same attitude. Prof. H. Van Oyen contends that, however horrible the crime of rape may be, we are never justified to counter it with another crime, namely infanticide. What is your opinion?

9. Comment on this warning issued by Dr. Vincent Collins of the Cook County Hospital: "Infanticide is just around the corner. From the fetus you go to infanticide, then you eliminate the old; you eliminate races. It [abortion] just opens up the whole Pandora's box of people control."

Q. *If a Communistic force seizes our government, must
the Christian obey these usurpers or may he revolt?
Does the apostle Paul shed light on this in Romans
13:1, 2?*

A. There is a certain finality and absoluteness in these
words of the apostle Paul. In saying, "Let *every soul* be
in subjection to the higher powers: for there is *no*
power but of God; and the powers *that be* are ordained
of God" he speaks universally and without qualification.
No exception is included in this passage. No matter
what the character of the highest ruler is; no matter how
the reins of government were secured (and Paul likely
wrote this when the infamous Nero was on the throne),
the ruler constitutes a "minister of God" (vs. 4) and
the Christian must obey, not merely because he will be
penalized if he doesn't, but for conscience sake — this
is his duty under God.

Paul's statement is a strong one and it would seem
to rule out such things as underground activities and a
sabotage movement. The *de facto* government must be
recognized as legally constituted by God. In His providence, God even allows evil rulers to come into power.
He may permit it in order to chastise a nation, and this
rebel government then is God's judgment on the
people.

There is a qualification, of course. This rebel government may forbid the preaching of the gospel. Then a

Christian must resist. He must then defy the government in this regulation, even as did Peter in a similar situation when he laid down the principle, "We must obey God rather than men" (Acts 5:29). But we contend that the common man, or the ordinary citizen, has no right to instigate revolution. If he did, it would mark the breakdown of all stability and order. The only way open to overthrow a tyrant is by enlisting the support of lesser magistrates: congressmen, governors, and so forth, and since they are legal possessors of authority, they may institute measures to replace a tyranical government.

Although this does not adequately dispose of all the thorny issues of this complex problem, it does lay down the Biblical principles that are to serve as a guide of conduct.

QUESTIONS

1. The late Dr. Martin Luther King promoted the doctrine of civil disobedience. He maintained that if a law was unjust, it ought to be disobeyed (in a nonviolent manner) because an unjust law is an immoral one. What do you think of this doctrine? Does it have Scriptural support?

2. Are there Biblical examples of revolution? Israel leaving Egypt (Exod. 12)? Edom throwing off the yoke of Israel (II Kings 8:20, 22; II Chron. 21:8, 10)?

3. At the time of the American Revolution it is estimated that 65 per cent of the Americans were Calvinists. Was this revolution justified? Were there religious reasons for it or simply political and economic ones?

4. If the government should decide that all of our children in America should go to public schools, what should parents who are committed to Christian education do?

5. If revolution is not a viable option for a Christian, what can and should a Christian do in order to remedy the evils in society?

6. How should we react and what measures should we

as Christians take against the New Left, who says that the Establishment is corrupt and our entire system must go?

7. What do you think of Calvin's advice to his fellow countrymen in France who were undergoing bitter persecution: "To your enemies fury oppose prayer and tears. God will not let one of them fall to the ground, but will put them in His bottle as He says in His psalm."

12 May a Christian Will His Body to Science?

Q. *May a Christian assign his body after his demise to medical science?*

A. A moral question like this has to be personally answered in the light of the Biblical teaching regarding the human body and regarding death.

Although man, as to his physical constitution, was made of inferior stuff or the lowly earth, his body is noble in that it partakes of the image of God; houses an immortal soul; in the case of the Christian becomes a "temple of the Holy Spirit"; and is designed for an eternal destiny in that reunion of body and soul in the resurrection.

In view of its nobility, the human body is not to be disparaged, neglected, or abused. And this care, respect, and concern would seem to carry over to the remains after the soul has departed. Then the body is no more than a shell, it is true; but its former associations and its future destiny would prevent it from being considered inconsequential and of no account. The past and future have implications for it, and it is more than mere animal matter. It may not be regarded as worthless and valueless.

As far as death is concerned, the Scriptures depict the corpse as a symbol of uncleanness and impurity in connection with its susceptibility to decay and decomposition (Lev. 21:11; Num. 6:6; 19:11-13); declare death to be a penalty of God since "the wages of sin is death" (Rom. 6:23); and view death as an enemy which all men must eventually face and which for the Christian has been conquered in principle in Christ (1 Cor. 15:55-57).

It is in the light of such Biblical teachings that the question must be answered.

We may look at it this way. If given over to science, the remains are not desecrated but dedicated to a legitimate and praiseworthy end. The purpose of such post-mortem dissection and exploration is to help our medical researchers locate the cause of death-dealing diseases, find an antidote to them, and prolong human life. This is not an attemept to nullify the penalty of God or outwit that great enemy death. I know that at the beginning of the modern medical science era such allegations were made, some of them by clergymen. The use of chloroform and inoculation for smallpox were condemned on religious grounds, the former being called a "decoy of Satan," offering itself so they said, "to bless women [it was first used in 1847 in the case of childbirth] but in the end it will harden society and rob God of the deep earnest cries which arise in time of trouble for help"; and the latter was called a "daring, profane violation of our holy religion." It was assumed that man must take these things as they come.

But better thinking prevailed. Men turned back to the "cultural mandate" of Genesis 1 and associated the "subduing of the earth" with advances in medical science. They took a second look at the second table of the law and bent themselves to the task of doing everything possible to better the physical lot and extend the lifespan of man. The principle of love prevailed. Pushing back the frontiers of disease and death was regarded as a gift of God's common grace. And many Christians now take the position that in giving their bodies to medical science the body is not being violated, God's commands are not being broken, and furthermore, this constitutes a contribution to the welfare of mankind.

It must be added, however, that from the nature of the case, the individual involved must make the ultimate decision. He is responsible to God for his own body. It is uniquely his under God; it houses his unique personality, and he must decide whether with clear conscience he may make this contribution to the promotion of medical science. If doubts plague him regarding such a decision, he had better refrain from making the pledge.

Questions

1. If the family and relatives have objections on sentimental grounds to devoting the corpse to science, who should make the final decision? Is the will of the person about to die to be determinative?

2. Does I Corinthians 6:20: "Glorify God in your body" speak to this question?

3. Does the doctrine of the Final Resurrection have any bearing on the question?

4. Millennia ago the Egyptians had developed the art of embalming to such a degree that bodies could be preserved intact for a long time. If this art is recovered, would that argue against postmortem use of the body for medical purposes?

5. Sometimes the accusation is made that our funerals, with their attendant expenses and practices, are essentially pagan. Do you agree? If so, how can they be made more Christian?

Is Pugilism a Permissible Sport? 13

Q. *What do you think of the sport of boxing?*

A. Legitimate sports serve a very wholesome purpose in life. They afford a fine recreation after a stint of hard work and a good release from the tensions of a rapid world. They build up the body so that it can be a better vehicle for the soul and they furnish a fine outlet for the vigor and enthusiasm of children and young people.

However, a sport must be evaluated from at least two points of view: one, the place it is permitted to occupy in our lives; and two, its specific goal or objective. It ought to be superfluous to say to Christians (but it is well to say it because of the imbalance and preoccupation with pleasure in our age) that sports and recreation must never become primary. If they do they become a sin. They must always remain secondary and serve a subsidiary purpose.

Paul says in I Timothy 4:8: "... bodily exercise is profitable for a little; but godliness is profitable for all things, having promise of the life which now is, and of that which is to come." Sports may never be permitted to absorb so much of our time and attention that they encroach upon the serious business of life.

Secondly, each sport must be judged and evaluated on the basis of its own specific goals and objectives. The question must be asked, What is the particular aim of this sport? To illustrate: The aim of baseball is to score runs by hitting the horsehide where the opposing team cannot lay hands on it; that of basketball to catapult the ball through the hoop more frequently than your opponents; of tennis to score points by accurate placements; of golf to direct the white pellet to the elusive cup in the least number of strokes; of football to prevent the other team from scoring but to carry the ball over your own goal line; and of bowling to avoid the gutters and, by unerring aim, sweep the pins from the pin deck.

In all of these instances the play is not directed primarily at the other person. Even in football where body contact is inevitable, that contact is incidental to the purpose of the game. The aim is to cross the goal line — not injure the opponent. Competition has to do with something outside of them. It is competition *with* rather than *against*. And that is legitimate. The apostle Paul undoubtedly witnessed foot races in his day and did not hesitate to use them as analogies of the Christian life (cf. II Timothy 2:5, etc.). The play was not focused upon the *person* of the opposition.

The case is far different in pugilism. Here the opponent, like the gladiator in the Roman arena, is the direct object of attack. It focuses upon the person directly. The aim is to incapacitate another human being who, mark well, is a fellow image-bearer of God. The objective is to hit him in vital and vulnerable points and either jar him into insensibility or reduce him to such state of physical disability that he can no longer continue the match. It is true that a medical examination must precede the bout and gloves cover the bare knuckles but that really has no bearing on the question. The objective is not a legitimate one. This is a brutal "sport" and there is no room for brutality in the Christian experience.

It is likewise a physically damaging "sport," one that has resulted in some 165 fatalities in the last fourteen years. If often does permanent injury to the pugilists and one who engages in it does so at great bodily risk to himself. Dr. T. Gorman, writing in the publication of the American Medical Association, excerpts of which appeared in an issue of the *Readers' Digest,* commented on the fact that a single hard blow to the head could and does cause death by massive cerebral hemorrhage. He said, "Boxing is the only sport where the head is the chief target, where the aim is to punish an opponent by knocking him out. But a boxer doesn't have to be knocked out or have his skull broken to be seriously injured. He may suffer pinpoint hemorrhages so that the harm to his brain is not apparent even to the trained physician."

Boxing hardly can be condoned or justified by the Christian. All men are image-bearers of God. All of them as creatures of God carry the marks and tokens of His handiwork. We are commanded to treat them with love and consideration, seeking their moral, spiritual and physical welfare. That would allow for wholesome competition, but it would not allow for the specific objective of affecting damage to him as a person. And that is implicit in boxing. Hence it constitutes a violation of the Biblical ethic, especially as it concerns our duties to our fellow men who, with us, are image-bearers of God.

Q. *Is the game of football permissible for the Christian?*

A. The evaluation of this particular sport would have to be made on the basis of *motivation involved* and the *incidence of injuries and fatalities.*

With respect to the first point, the motivation of the game of football is sound and there is no room for criticism on that score. The aim of the game is simply to get the ball over the goal line or between the goalposts. The team that does this the greatest number of times registers the most points and wins. Football is in an entirely different class from boxing which we considered in the previous section. There the intent is to pummel the opponent to the point of exhaustion and physical incapacity so that he is no longer able to "lift his dukes" and protect himself. To batter and bruise a fellow image-bearer in that way and for that purpose is clearly wrong. Boxing cannot be justified on the score of proper motivation. But football can.

With respect to injuries and fatalities, the judgment becomes more difficult. All of the sports have risks involved and possibilities of injuries and fatalities. There are skull fractures and broken bones in ice hockey when players collide or are driven into the boards in their attempt to control the puck. Basketball has its sprains, bruises, and broken limbs, and baseball has its "bean balls." In such a contact sport as football it is plausible to assume that injuries and fatalities would be more numerous than in some of the other sports. But only if a complete body of statistics were gathered, that is, only when we know the percentage of injuries and fatalities in comparison with the total number of players participating and make a comparison with other sports, can a valid judgment be made.

But does not this sport fall under the strictures of the confessional writings which interpret the sixth commandment as making it incumbent upon me that "I harm not myself nor willfully expose myself to any danger"? This objection seems invalid because all available precautions are taken.

A complete physical examination is a requirement; the uniforms are equipped with heavy padding; there is a helmet and face protector; and there are heavy penalties imposed for personal fouls and clipping. It is true that one has to be in superb physical condition to participate. A 165-pounder would find it a "breathtaking" experience if a few 250-pounders landed on him. But the game can hardly be interpreted as wilful exposure to danger and risk of life and limb. This description would apply to acrobats performing their death-defying stunts on the high trapeze with no net underneath, but it would not apply to playing football.

References have been made, too, to injuries that are sustained in stack-ups where "dirty," unscrupulous players jab with their elbows and try to physically incapacitate their opponents who are under the heap with them. Mention is made, too, of coaches who instruct their players to "go out and get him," that is, try to put out of commission a player on the opposing team. This is indefensible and deplorable, of course. But it is no criticism of the *game*. It is an abuse of it. Here is another good opportunity to show Christianity in action. A certain football player has said that it was a refreshing, wholesome experience to play against the Wheaton College team. What impressed him was the Christian sportsmanship exhibited. "Dirty" tactics were conspicuously absent, and it was a clean, hard-fought game.

The money involved in fielding a football team is an important factor to consider. Stewardship of our financial resources is a sacred duty that devolves upon us. There is much wisdom in the words of Senator Byrd of Virginia, who, when he was asked about our astronomical expenditure of money to finance a flight to the moon, said: "I favor it only on the *pay as you go plan*." This could also be applied to football in high schools and colleges.

Questions

1. Paul predicts that in the last days men will be "lovers of pleasure rather than lovers of God" (II Tim. 3:4). Do you think that this characterizes our day?

2. Does Paul's reference to Greek games (I Cor. 9:24, etc.) contain any implications as to his view of sports? What did he mean in I Corinthians 9:27 when he said: "I pommel my body and subdue it, lest after preaching to others I myself should be disqualified" (RSV)?

3. It is said that "The family that prays together and that plays together stays together." Do you agree? What family recreations should we engage in?

4. Does the fact that a Christian's body is the temple of the Holy Spirit have any implications for a physical fitness program for the Christian? What guidelines should he follow?

5. Are cigarette smoking and alcoholic consumption drawbacks to a physical fitness program? If the Christian is committed to the duty of keeping his body in excellent physical condition so that it can serve as a fit vehicle for the soul, do you consider the above-named practices sinful?

6. What do you think of the late John F. Kennedy's judgment in *The Soft American*: "Physical fitness is not only one of the most important keys to a healthy body, it is the basis of dynamic and creative intellectual activity. The relationship between the soundness of the body and the activities of the mind is subtle and complex. Much is not yet understood. But we know what the Greeks knew — that intelligence and skill can only function at the peak of their capacity when the body is healthy and strong; that hardy spirits and tough minds usually inhabit sound bodies"?

7. What about stewardship of our resources? May a Christian purchase an expensive yacht or speedboat or pay high membership fees at a country club, assuming that he does not neglect giving his tithe to the Kingdom?

8. There are Christian athletes in professional sports. They play on Sunday but witness to others during the days of the week. Bobby Richardson, former great second baseman for the New York Yankees, speaks at evangelistic rallies. Kermit Zarley, professional golfer, leads a Bible study group (involving some twenty-five professional golfers who play regularly on the tour) during the week because matches are normally played on Sunday. What is your reaction to this? Charlie Maxwell, former outfielder for the Detroit Tigers, once defended his Sunday play on the ground that God had given him this particular talent and expected him to use it. What is our responsibility as viewers of the athletic contests and sports events in person and on T.V.?

THE INCARNATION AND ATONEMENT
OF JESUS CHRIST

Q. *Was Mary of the Davidic line?*

A. The two genealogies in the Gospels are not easy to interpret and reconcile.

Certain differences in the two genealogies are explainable since Matthew and Luke beam their writings to different readers. Matthew writes particularly for the Jews; he therefore goes back to their esteemed forebears, David and Abraham. Luke writes primarily for the Gentile world; hence he goes back to Adam, the head of the whole human race.

There are those who think that we have Joseph's descent in Matthew (he goes back then to David's son, Solomon) while we have Mary's descent in Luke (and she goes back to another son of David, namely Nathan). This view has been held by reputable scholars: Meyer, Wieseler, and others.

But other scholars (for instance, John Calvin and Dean Alford) hold that both Gospel writers are dealing only with the ancestral line of Joseph. One of them, Matthew, traces Joseph's legal and royal descent because he wants to stress the fact that Christ the king is descended from a line of kings. The other Gospel writer, Luke, traces His natural descent.

If, however, both deal with Joseph, how do you account for the different names that occur in the genealogies and how do you establish the fact that Mary also was of the line of David?

The answer of those who hold this view is as follows: It was not at all unusual for the same man to bear different names, and likely there are two different names for the same individual in these family lines. And what about Mary? Calvin says that the law insisted that each one must marry within his own tribe, and therefore if Joseph was of the tribe of Judah and descended from David, so too was Mary. Several Biblical passages, notably Luke 1:32; Acts 2:30; Romans 1:3; II Timothy 2:8; and Revelation 5:5, substantiate the truth that Jesus was descended from David of the tribe of Judah.

Questions

1. What meaning must be attached to the words of the angel to Mary as recorded in Luke 1:28-30? How honorable a position does Mary occupy?

2. What can you conclude as to the character of Mary from Luke 1:38 and 2:19?

3. Did Mary show undue solicitude for her Son (who is, after all, divine) when she feared that He was overworking Himself (Mark 3:31-35)? Or was this but natural on her part?

4. The tribe that was set aside for the priestly work in the Old Testament was the tribe of Levi. Jesus, the Messiah, was the great High Priest. But He was descended from David who came from the tribe of Judah. Would this invalidate Jesus for His priestly work of atonement?

5. Is the Virgin Birth doctrine significant for the Christian faith? (See Isa. 7:14; Matt. 1:18, 20; Luke 1:34, 35; and Gal. 4:4).

6. The late Karl Barth accepted the doctrine of the Virgin Birth. According to him, the "sin-inheritance" (the sin we get from Adam) is passed on by the male parent and Jesus received "creatureliness" (He became truly human) by being born of Mary but He escaped the "sin-inheritance"

since Joseph was merely His foster-father. What do you think of this view?

7. Comment on this quotation from Father John Hardin of Notre Dame: "In the degree which a person believes that Mary was immaculately conceived, that she is the Mother of God, and is now gloriously reigning in heaven, body and soul, interceding for us with her divine Son, to that extent he is truly Christian. Insofar as he deviates from these Marian doctrines and worse still, shows himself hostile to those who believe in them, we do not question his sincerity, but we say that he has departed from the gospel of Christ and is alien to its spirit of Christianity" (*Christian Century,* Nov. 13, 1963, p. 1406).

15 Was Mary a Teen-ager at Jesus' Birth?

Q. *When Jesus was born was his mother Mary in her early teens?*

A. We have no means of knowing for certain. No ages are recorded in the Gospel records.

The main source for the above view is an apocryphal New Testament book by the name of *Protevangelion* and reputedly written by James the Less, the brother of Christ. It records that when Mary was twelve years of age the priests in the temple entered into consultation and, having received command of an angel, they sought a widower as husband for Mary. By the casting of the lot Joseph was chosen, and even though he protested at first saying, "I am an old man, and have children . . . and I fear lest I should appear ridiculous in Israel" (8:13), he was dissuaded and he agreed to marry her. She was taken into his home and at the age of fourteen, so the *Protevangelion* states, conceived by the Holy Spirit, and in due time brought forth the Messiah.

It is this fictional and therefore unreliable source that is the basis of the above contention.

As far as the Scriptures are concerned, they fail to make mention of Joseph after that episode in the temple when Jesus, at the age of twelve, amazed the learned men of his day by his astuteness of understanding. Some have concluded from this that Joseph must have been considerably older than Mary when they entered into holy matrimony. It may be, however, that he died young and hence he disappears from the record.

1. What did Simeon mean by his prediction to Mary: "Behold, this child is set for the fall and rising of many in Israel, and for a sign that is spoken against (and a sword will pierce through your own soul also), that thoughts out of many hearts may be revealed" (Luke 2:34-35, RSV)?

2. How would you characterize Jesus' attitude towards His mother as is evident in Luke 2:49 and John 2:4? Does this differ from the attitude He shows in John 19:26-27?

3. Was Mary aware of her own sinfulness? (See Luke 1:47; Acts 1:14; etc.) How does this compare with the views expressed by Knox-Cox, a Roman Catholic, who calls Mary the second Eve as Christ is the Second Adam and writes: "Just as Eve brought shame on womanhood by her transgression, so Mary has reestablished the glorious position of womanhood by her obedience"? Does this make of Mary a Co-Redeemer?

4. Comment on this quotation from the late Pope John XXIII: "Ours is a Marian age and it becomes more evident day by day that the way for men to return to God is by Mary; and Mary is the basis of our confidence, the guarantee of our security, the foundation of our hope. The modern development of Mariology and Marian piety in the church is the surest sign and the happiest forecast that Mary is the greatest help offered us by God for the attainment of unity."

16 Did Jesus Have a Human Soul?

Q. Did Jesus have a human soul?

A. We are involved here in the mystery of the personality of our Lord, and consequently we admit at the outset that our answer has definite limitations.

One of the faculties of the soul is the intellect or mind. In His divine nature Jesus, of course, knew all things. He could penetrate the recesses of a man's soul. "He himself knew what was in man" (John 2:25). As divine, He knew the future. "Jesus, therefore, knowing all the things that were coming upon him . . ." (John 18:4). But in His human nature, His knowledge was limited. With respect to the date of His second coming He said, "But of that day and hour knoweth no one, not even the angels of heaven, neither the Son, but the Father only" (Matt. 24:36).

Another faculty of the soul is the will. In His divine nature, Jesus says, as the Psalmist predicts it, "Lo, I am come . . . I delight to do thy will, O my God" (Ps. 40:7-8); but in the intensity of His sufferings in the Garden, when the anticipation of coming anguish is almost overpowering, He says in His human nature, "If it be possible, let this cup pass away from me: nevertheless, not as I will, but as thou wilt" (Matt. 26:39).

This does not mean that Jesus becomes a split personality. He remains a unified and integrated person. But there is this diversity in His reactions. That leads us to conclude that Jesus as the true man had a human soul. And that is about all that can be said on the subject.

Questions

1. Why was it necessary for Christ to be truly human? (See John 12:27; Acts 3:18; Heb. 2:14; 9:22; etc.)

2. Did Jesus catch colds as a boy and contract the usual childhood diseases? Did He feel attraction for the opposite sex? What is the nature of His normal development as described in Luke 2:52?

3. Jesus used the title *Son of Man* over forty times in His ministry. Why did He prefer that title for Himself?

4. In the main Jesus speaks of Himself in single terms, that is, He refers to Himself as *I* and *me* (e.g. John 10:30; Matt. 27:46). In John 3:11, however, there appears to be a plural usage. Why is this the case?

5. Of what practical value in our everyday life is it for us as Christians that our Saviour and Lord was true man?

6. Comment on this evaluation of Jesus by a contemporary theologian, Nels Ferre: "We know that Jesus had weaknesses, ignorance, finitude, mortality. We know that he had real temptations of great depth and power.... Jesus in the most natural and indirect instances seems to have been humbly conscious of sin before God.... Jesus learned from the struggles of his moral conflicts.... Jesus as a human being was born again, and experienced rapture and new levels of acceptance by God" (*Christ and the Christian,* pp. 110-112).

17 Was the Human Nature of Jesus Omnipotent?

Q. *Is it true that Christ's divine nature was omnipotent but not his human nature?*

A. That is separating the two natures unduly.

Do not fail to remember that Christ is but one person. As the Second Person of the Trinity in eternity He was one person, and He remained that when He took on a human nature. He is now the God-man.

And we may not take these attributes and parcel them out between Christ's two natures. If we do, we lose the unity of His person and operate with a double personality. As God-man Jesus is omnipotent, omniscient, and so forth. It is true that He did not use His divine powers as a boy. But He was divine nonetheless. He held this divine power in reserve until He launched His public ministry at the age of thirty. Then He exercised it, showing infinite power over every sphere.

It is very true that we are dealing here with a mystery. The union of two natures in one personality defies comprehension. We must, however, guard against misconceptions. And one of them is to separate the two natures so radically that the unity of the Person is lost.

Questions

1. One way in which Jesus showed His omnipotence and His sovereignty was by the performance of miracles. Over what various spheres did He show His wondrous power?

What do you think was the crowning miracle of Jesus' career?

2. For what various purposes did Jesus perform miracles?

3. On the basis of the prediction made in Isaiah 53:2b the contention is made that Jesus' body was deformed. Is there basis for that thought in the text? How is this to be related to the requirements laid down in the Mosaic law with respect to sacrifices? If an animal had something defective, might he be used as a sacrifice?

4. How can you reconcile the omnipotence of Christ with the fact that upon occasion He became fatigued, hungry, and thirsty?

5. How do you account for the fact that in some cases Jesus enjoined silence of the one whom He had healed (e.g. Mark 1:40-45)? Wouldn't you think that He would expect the healed man to be a witness of His saving power?

6. What do you think of Van Buren's description of Christ: "He was free from anxiety and the need to establish His own identity, but He was above all free for His neighbor.... He was apparently a man free to give Himself to others whoever they were. He lived thus and He was put to death for being this kind of man in the midst of fearful and defensive men" (*The Secular Meaning of the Gospel*, p. 123).

18 How Complete Was Jesus' Knowledge When He Was Here upon Earth?

Q. *Was Jesus omniscient (all knowing) when He was here upon earth?*

A. It appears upon occasion that there was no limitation upon Jesus' knowledge.

He foretold the betrayal of Judas and the coming denial of Peter. Before the Lord's Supper was instituted He ordered Peter and John to precede them into the city and make the proper preparations. He told them that they would meet a man bearing a pitcher who would direct them to the feast chamber, and He even disclosed to them the conversation that would ensue. The Gospel writer, John, does not hesitate to say that Jesus could penetrate into our inner recesses because "He himself *knew what was in man*" (John 2:25). The same writer tells us that as the passion program was beginning to unfold "Jesus, therefore, *knowing all the things that were coming upon Him, went forth . . .*" (John 18:4). Thus it seems as though there are no limits to His knowledge.

There is another side to the picture however. When Matthew relates the farewell discourses of our Lord and refers to the time of the Second Coming, he quotes Jesus as saying: "But of that day and hour knoweth no one, not even the angels of heaven, *neither the Son,* but the Father only" (Matt. 24:36).

How are we to understand these passages? It seems

that even though we may not separate Jesus' two natures to such an extent that we lose the unity of His personality, we shall have to enunciate this twofold truth: one, that as the Son of God He did possess knowledge of everything, past, present, and future; but also that as the Son of God who became man and was born under the law, He placed himself under the law, he placed himself under certain limitations — such limitations that even though He was omnipotent He became weary and fatigued, and even though He was omniscient He was ignorant of some things.

QUESTIONS

1. There is no doubt of the fact that Jesus was aware already at an early age that He was the promised Messiah (Luke 2:49). Some claim that after a period of meditation He arrived at that conviction; others that, since the people of His day were expecting a Messiah, He determined to be one. Was this conviction innate within Him? Or, how did He get it?

2. What characterized Jesus as a prophet or teacher? (Cf. Matt. 7:28-29; Luke 4:22; etc.)

3. Jesus claimed unique knowledge of the Father (John 10:15, etc.). What did He mean by this claim?

4. Do you think that Jesus was exceptionally bright as a youngster? (See Luke 2:47.) It is implied in Luke 2:52 that He underwent the normal educational processes. Does this mean that it took real effort on His part to acquire knowledge? Or, since He was the Son of God, was there really no need for Him to undergo the regular schooling of His day?

5. What did Jesus mean by telling His disciples, "Ye shall know the truth and the truth shall make you free" (John 8:32)? Does the context indicate what kind of freedom He has in mind? We speak of a *liberal* arts education. Is its intention also to give freedom?

6. As teacher, Jesus laid down some rather unusual

teachings. One of them is found in the Parable of the Unjust Steward (Luke 16:1-9). What do you think was the main intent of Jesus in this parable?

7. Evaluate this comment from Georgia Harkness: "If one believes, he will affirm belief in Christ as the Son of God. This does not mean that Jesus was God. It means that His life was so filled with the character and power of God that when men have seen Him, they have seen the Father" (*Understanding the Christian Faith*).

Was Jesus a Nazirite or an Essene? **19**

Q. *Was Jesus either a Nazirite or an Essene?*

A. The evidence is very much against it.

According to Numbers 6:3ff. the vow that the Nazirite took involved a pledge to refrain from the use of wine or strong drink and any product of the grapevine, to allow his hair to grow without setting a razor to it, and to avoid contact with a corpse. It appears that this vow was taken for a restricted period of time. The term *Nazirite* means *one separated*.

There is no indication in the Gospels that our Lord ever took such a vow. It is true that He is called a Nazarene (Matt. 2:23, etc.), but that simply means that He was a citizen of Nazareth. And how and why Nazareth, which has the same root meaning of separation as Nazirite, adopted that name as the designation for that little community, we have no means of knowing.

What about the Essenes?

The Essenes or the Qumran sect, details of which came to light in the discovery of the Dead Sea Scrolls in 1947, lived on the shores of the Dead Sea. And although there are some surface similarities between that sect and the Christian community, the differences between them are fundamental and basic. There is no trace in Essene teaching of a doctrine of Incarnation or Atonement, both of which are pivotal in Christianity.

The *Teacher of Righteousness* who plays a major role in the Qumran setup made no claim to Messiahship, nor did others ascribe it to him. This was a monastic and communistic community, and Jesus — as we know — commended a life in society and assumed the right of private property. (His words to the rich young ruler must not be viewed as a permanent, universal rule. He was simply rebuking that man for making goods into a god.) As far as we know, Jesus never had contact with this group, and His basic life and teachings are diametrically opposed to them.

Questions

1. The Nazirite (most of whom took the vow for a limited time although Samuel, Samson, and John the Baptist took it permanently) committed himself to a separated life. Why was this necessary within the life of the covenant people?

2. Jesus called His followers to live a separate life "in, but not of, the world." How can we carry out this command of our Lord without withdrawal? In what must our separation consist? Is this a matter of ideals and goals? actions?

3. The purported quotation in Matthew 2:23 "that He might be called a Nazarene" cannot be located in the Old Testament. Is this a misquotation? Could it possibly be a reference to Isaiah 1:1 where the word *branch* is derived from a Hebrew word *netzer*? If so, is this merely a play on words?

4. The *Teacher of Righteousness* in Essene literature was a confessed sinner who gratefully acknowledged dependence upon God for forgiveness, taught his followers to hate their enemies, performed no works of healing or compassion, and started a legalistic community on the outside. Show from the Gospels (e.g. Matt. 5:43) how this differs radically from the New Testament portrait of Jesus.

5. There are liberal scholars who maintain that we have no reliable picture of Jesus in the New Testament. He lived

around A.D. 30 and the Gospels were not written until thirty or forty years later. In that intervening period there were stories about Him and His works in the various Christian communities. This was called "oral tradition." But these stories differed (note the differences between Matthew, Mark, and Luke) and consequently we cannot be sure that the Christ of faith is the same as the Jesus of history. How would you answer such an argument?

6. Comment on this quotation from John Knox's *On the Meaning of Christ* (1945): "Christ is of one substance with the Father but the utmost and the inmost it is given us to know of God's substance is that He is love ... and love is not a metaphysical substance but personal moral will and action."

20 When Did Jesus' Flight into Egypt Occur?

Q. *In the light of Luke 2:39, when did Jesus' flight into Egypt occur?*

A. The answer must be sought in the fact that not one of the Gospel writers purports to give a complete history of the life of our Lord. Each one, under the Spirit's leading, includes only that which is necessary for his own purpose.

Matthew, for instance, says nothing about the circumcision nor the presentation ceremonies, but he does tell about the adoration of Magi and about the terrible slaughter engineered by wicked Herod, neither of which finds mention in the book of Luke. These are not unintentional omissions and insertions but are to be understood in the light of the purposes of the authors.

Consequently, if we would reconstruct those early events, using both Gospels which provide information, it would seem to follow this course: Jesus was born in the manger of an accessory building to the inn (Luke 2:7) where He was worshiped by the Jewish shepherds. Then, apparently, Joseph and Mary secured better quarters in the city (Matt. 2:11), and it was there that the Gentile Magi made their obeisance. Before the Magi came to lay the treasures of the Gentile world at his feet, Jesus was circumcised (Luke 2:21) and presented in the temple on the fortieth day as the law prescribed (Luke 2:22ff.). Then, upon the departure of the Wise

Men (the angel warning Joseph about the death decree about to be issued by Herod, who feared that there was a serious competitor for his throne), Joseph and Mary packed their belongings and, leaving under cover of night, took refuge in Egypt, remaining there until the death of Herod (Matt. 2:15). It may well be, then, that Jesus was a few years old before they returned to Nazareth and reinstated themselves there.

In other words, the events recorded by Matthew in Chapter 2 fit chronologically between Luke 2:38 and Luke 2:39.

Questions

1. Matthew and Luke have infancy accounts of Jesus. Mark and John do not. Why are they missing in the latter?

2. Jesus was to be born a great prophet, and Athens was the center of wisdom and learning; a great king, and Rome was the political center of the world; and a great priest, and Jerusalem was the religious center. Isn't it strange that Jesus was not born in one of those great cities rather than in small and obscure Bethlehem?

3. Where did the Magi come from? Is there any religious significance in the kinds of gifts that they brought?

4. Circumcision was a symbol of the "cutting away of sin." But Jesus was sinless. Why then was He forced to submit to the rite of circumcision? Were His parents unaware of His sinlessness?

5. What sort of ceremony was the presentation in the temple (Luke 2)? What meaning did it have and what predictions were made on that occasion by Simeon and Anna?

6. Besides the infancy accounts, the only events recorded in the Gospels about Jesus in His first thirty years are the flight into Egypt and the episode in the temple at the age of twelve. Are we to conclude from this fact that those thirty years were, in the main uneventful and unimportant? Why

did He wait until the age of thirty to begin His public ministry? Is this related to the age at which the priest began to serve in the Old Testament economy?

Could Jesus Sin? **21**

Q. *Could Jesus sin? If He could not sin, was not His temptation an invalid one?*

A. There is no doubt that our Lord was really tempted. The Gospel writers make it clear that when Jesus met the devil in the wilderness, this was no figure of speech or an apparent testing. This was for real. And the author of the letter to the Hebrews verifies this when he tells us that "he [Jesus] himself hath suffered being tempted" (2:18). The reality of the temptations of Christ is not open to question.

But the question will not down. If Jesus was not able to sin (and since He is God He is therefore immune to sin), what could be the force of the temptation? Does not temptation imply both the possibility of standing and of falling? Does it not logically follow that if one cannot sin, temptation can have no real significance for him? And does it not stand to reason that temptation, to be authentic, must carry with it the possibiliy of falling into sin?

There is nothing wrong with that logic.

But we cannot use the rational approach. We must adopt the religious. Ours is the perspective of faith.

And faith implies acceptance of the givens of Scripture.

The Bible tells us that Satan tempted Jesus as the God-man. The point of contact was His human nature.

Since He was truly man, He could be and was truly tempted. The urge to evil was real. To resist and turn down the overtures of the devil involved a struggle of soul (Heb. 2:18). There was deliberate rejection of the actual allurements of the Evil One. But we must add, as the Scriptures do, that when the temptation passed through the human nature and reached the divine Person, it was stymied. Hence we stand before this paradox of the Scriptures: Jesus was really tempted and Jesus was unable to sin.

Questions

1. When Peter says about Christ "Who did not sin, neither was guile found in his mouth" (I Peter 2:22) did he possibly mean that Christ could have sinned but actually did not do so?

2. Were there sinless men in history before Christ? Both Noah (Gen. 6:9) and Job (Job 1:1) are called *perfect*. Does that mean that they were without sin? (Cf. Gen. 9:21; Job 42:6.) Or does perfection here mean something other than sinlessness?

3. What was the essence of the temptation that Jesus experienced in the wilderness (Matt. 4; Luke 4)? Wherein lay the inducement to sin? Was there something inherently wrong in Jesus making stones into bread? Or in jumping from the pinnacle of the temple? Would the sin (in case Jesus had given in) have resided in the fact that it was Satan who was throwing out the invitation? Was Satan possibly urging Jesus to get the Kingdom in ways other than that ordained by God?

4. When Luke tells us that the Devil "departed from him [Jesus] for a season" (4:13b) he implies that there were other temptations in the life of our Lord. Do you discern a temptation on the Mount of Transfiguration? in the Garden of Gethsemane?

5. Schleiermacher, the theologian, claimed that Christ had a perfect and unbroken sense of communion with God

so that He asked at all times: "What would God want me to do?" If he is correct, does this explain why Jesus never fell into sin? If we had that sense of communion, could we also live without sinning?

6. What do you think of this quotation from Emil Brunner, a Neo-Orthodox writer: "To them [the New Testament writers] He [Jesus] is no religious genius but a Saviour; no founder of a new religion, but one in whom God Himself is present among men ... the eternally contemporary word of God present and alive today, the reality of God in a godless world" (*Christian Century,* Dec. 23, 1931, p. 1622)?

22 Who Crucified Christ?

Q. *Vatican II has gone on record saying that the Jews were not guilty of crucifying our Lord. Is this Biblical?*

A. The late Pope John XXIII introduced the subject in the Vatican II Council. He was much concerned about anti-Semitism and hatred of the Jews in the world and thought it highly necessary to make a judgment on it. And he was quite right. The Jew throughout history has been the target of ridicule and the object of injustice and discrimination.

After considerable discussion the Council made two pronouncements. One is that the Jew today is exempted from special guilt in the death of Christ. The other is that, in a profound theological sense, all mankind is to blame for the crucifixion of our Lord.

We would concur in both of these judgments.

But something else needs to be said. And the Council was silent on it. It is undeniable that the Jews were immediately responsible. James Parkes, Paul Winter, and other liberals who maintain that the Romans alone were responsible and that the story of Jewish participation in the crucifixion is a later invention stemming from the hatred of the church for the synagogue, are dead wrong. The New Testament (see Acts 2:23; 3:15, 17, etc.) clearly teaches that the Jews, through their chief priests and scribes, played a major role in handing Jesus over to the Romans for trial and crucifixion. It is true that sin blinded their eyes and they did it in ignorance (John 12:40; Acts 3:17), but they did it nonetheless. Special guilt does attach to the Jews of Jesus' day.

But having said this, the other judgments are in order. Jews today must not be made the scapegoats. It is true that the Jewish leaders shouted recklessly: "His blood be upon us *and upon our children.*" But did they have the power to invoke this curse on their descendants? And is it to rest on them indefinitely? Furthermore, as some Bible scholars have pointed out, the blood of Christ falls on men not in revenge but only in forgiveness.

The other judgment is true also. All of us share in the blame for the death of Christ — not merely the Jews. Gentiles enter the transaction, too. We find this indicated in the Apostles' Creed in the article, "suffered under Pontius Pilate." All of mankind must assume its share of the blame because all of mankind fell into sin and our Lord came to bear the sin of the world. To summarize: the Jews and the Roman authorities of Jesus' day were directly responsible, but everyone was also involved; and it is decidedly unjust to lay the guilt at the door of one segment of the human race.

QUESTIONS

1. Pilate declared on at least three separate occasions that Jesus was innocent. And yet he condemned Jesus to death. That was a flagrant miscarriage of justice. It should not have occurred. But if Pilate had released Jesus upon declaring Him innocent, would there have been atonement for God's people?

2. Isn't it surprising that a low-grade politician like Pilate finds mention in the Apostles Creed which has now been recited by Christians for over nineteen hundred years? ·

3. Since the Jews as a nation did not recognize Jesus of

Nazareth as the Messiah, they called for His crucifixion. Will the time come when the scales will be removed and Jews will recognize Him as Saviour and Lord? (Cf. Rom. 11:17-27.)

4. How would you answer a man who says: "Had I been there when Jesus was crucified I would have tried to prevent it. At least I would have led a protest. I would have marched with signs protesting the great injustice that was being perpetrated"?

5. Is the hymn "Were You There When They Crucified My Lord?" doctrinally sound?

6. Romans were implicated in the death of Jesus; so were the Jews; and so were we. Is that a sample of the interlinking in historical events? Could we say that Russia, North Vietnam, South Vietnam, and the United States are all responsible for the tragedy in southeast Asia? Is this an illustration of the truth that John Donne stated when he said that "No man [nor nation] is an island"?

Did God Die on the Cross? **23**

Q. *If Jesus is in essence one with the Father and the Spirit, are we justified in speaking of the death of the Son of God?*

A. If the Father, Son and Spirit are one — which They are — then the death of one of Them would seem to involve the death of the other two members of the Trinity also. In that case God did die when the Lord expired on the cross.

We are dealing here with an incomprehensible mystery. It is one that transcends human reason. Only once in history did the Deity take on a human nature. And never again will it occur. This event is absolutely unique, and all attempts to rationalize it will inevitably fail.

The doctrinal standards show meticulous care and precision. They do not state that when Jesus said on Calvary, "It is finished," God died on the cross. The Scriptures are clear on that point. The divine cannot be extinguished. The Deity cannot die. But neither do the confessions say that Jesus as a human being died on Golgotha. That would give the impression that the divine and the human in Him were neatly separated when He came to His cross, and it was the human half that died. That would be to make of Jesus a split personality.

In the incarnation, the Second Person of the Holy

Trinity took on a human nature. This did not involve attaching another person to Himself. The human nature of Christ does not constitute another person. But on the other hand, it is not correct to say either that this human nature was impersonal. Neither of these views is supported by the Scriptures. In assuming a human nature, the Lord still constituted but one personality. In becoming the Mediator, He who existed only in a divine nature prior to the incarnation, remained a unipersonality. He became the God-man.

It is this truth that the doctrinal standards are seeking to express. The writers were aware of the fact that in the course of history the two natures of Christ had been separated so radically as to yield two persons. The Nestorians did that in the early centuries, and their views were condemned in the Council of Ephesus held in A.D. 431.

It is quite apparent what has to be avoided and what has to be maintained. The divinity may not be involved in dying, since that is an impossibility. And on the other hand the divine nature may not be cut asunder from the human when the great transaction of redemption occurs. The authors of the confession try to avoid those erroneous views by speaking of the "death of the Son of God" on the cross. In so doing, they give priority to the divine (after all, Christ did possess a divine nature before the human was conjoined to it) and speak in the vein of Titus 2:10 where Christ is designated "God our Saviour." They distinguish Christ as Son of God from the other two members of the Trinity, and thus preclude any view that the entire Godhead expired on the cross of Calvary. And they stress the unity of the personality of the Mediator. There is but one Person making atonement for the sins of His people.

In analyzing the statement from the confessions in

this way, it may appear that we are engaging in the very kind of rationalizing that was repudiated in the first part of this article. But that is hardly the case. The revered fathers of Dort were well aware of the mystery with which they were compelled to cope in their exposition of Christian doctrine. And they tried as best they could to ward off deviant views and at the same time do justice to all the data of the sacred Scriptures. The terminology they came up with may leave something to be desired. After all, they were as fallible as we are; but so long as we cannot register improvement upon them, we had better follow in their wake.

QUESTIONS

1. Did Jesus as Son of God die on the cross for the souls of men? Or did He also die for their bodies? (See Isa. 53, etc.)

2. Crucifixion is almost if not entirely extinct as a method of execution. Why is that the case? Has mankind become more humane in its actions?

3. One of the early Christian movements tried to explain the relationship of the two natures in Christ by the analogy of man and wife. As man and wife become one when they marry, so the two natures of Christ were joined as one when He became incarnate. What do you think of that analogy?

4. There are some modern theologians who maintain that Christ never taught the doctrine of substitutionary atonement (Christ dying in the place of His own) and that it was an invention of the apostle Paul. Can you find texts that disprove this contention? (See Matt. 26:28; Mark 10:45; etc.)

5. Those who hold that Christ gave His life for everyone in the world (general atonement doctrine) point to such texts as John 3:16 and Romans 5:18 where the terms *world* and *all men* are used. The question is: Do these words always mean every single individual? (Cf. Luke 2:1; Acts 11:28; 17:6; Rom. 1:8; etc.)

6. Comment on these quotations from Knudson: "In God Himself there never was any obstacle to man's redemption. There never was any need of reconciling God to the world. The only obstacle to man's redemption has always lain in man himself, and the only problem connected with his redemption has been that of his moral and spiritual transformation. . . ." "The death of Christ was a revealer of the sacrificial and righteous love of God. . . ." "The sacrificial love of God awakens an answering love in the hearts of men. This is the only way man can be redeemed, namely through moral and spiritual transformation. No other kind of redemption would be truly Christian."

What Is Meant by Descent into Hell? **24**

Q. *How did the descent into hell article find a place in the Apostles' Creed?*

A. It is true, of course, that the statement itself occurs nowhere in Scripture.

And the origin of the Apostles' Creed is shrouded in some mystery. It seems to be the precipitate of early confessions of faith. When catechumens in the early church had completed their course of study, they made confession of faith by reciting their basic beliefs. It appears that these early confessions eventually found fixed form in the fourth century and came to be known as the Apostles' Creed because this statement summarized the convictions of the apostles. One of the earliest references to this "descent into hell" article occurs in the creed of the Synod of Nice that was held in Thrace A.D. 359.

There has been a great deal of discussion and much difference of opinion about this article.

One area of difference is that of the meaning of the term. Some took it to be a translation of Sheol or Hades, meaning the "abode of the dead." Others said it was a translation of Gehenna and therefore betokened "hell." If the former, it has reference to Christ's burial and simply means that He "descended into the grave." That interpretation was helped by Chrysostom, Ignatius, Theophylact, and in Reformation times by Bucer and

Beza. The second interpretation was held in the Middle Ages by such men as Nicholas of Cusa and Pico Della Mirandola, and particularly by John Calvin who insisted that "a place must be given to this article, as it contains a useful and not to be despised mystery of a most important matter." In the *Institutes* he calls it "the invisible and incomprehensible vengeance that He (Christ) suffered from the hands of God" (I, 2, 16). The Apostles' Creed, so Calvin argues, first points out what Christ suffered in the sight of men and then that which He suffered in the sight of God. The "descent into hell" article is the latter, and it indicates the deeper significance of the passion of Christ.

As far as the proof texts adduced to support this position are concerned, in the main they are pertinent. Matthew 26:38, with its admission of being "sorrowful ... unto death"; Matthew 27:46 with its cry of forsakenness on the cross; and Hebrews 5:7 with its "strong crying and tears" are supportive of the basic teaching.

QUESTIONS

1. There are those who maintain that the Apostles' Creed is so called because its twelve articles were written by the twelve apostles, each one of them contributing one article. Do you think this is a likely theory?

2. In our century Christians are much concerned about uniting with other Christians. Churches are holding dialogues to see if they cannot bury their differences and form one organization. This movement is called *ecumenicity*. If the movement is Biblical — and Jesus did pray in His high-priestly prayer that His followers might be one (John 17) — would the Apostles Creed be a good basis upon which to unite?

3. Castellio, a teacher in the Geneva schools in the sixteenth century, refused to accept the Calvinistic interpretation of the article, "He descended into hell," and was banished by the city council from the city. Do you think that

action was too harsh? Does the time in which it happened give some explanation of that action?

4. Evaluate the following interpretations of this article of the Creed. Is there possible Biblical basis for the varying interpretations?

a. *Roman Catholic:* The Old Testament saints did not have complete salvation since Christ had not yet come. They could not go directly to heaven when they died and had to remain in a waiting room, called the *Limbus Patrum.* They were released and given access to heaven when Christ "descended into hell." Hell, then, is to be understood as the chamber in which the Old Testament saints were awaiting final redemption.

b. *Lutheran:* Christ's descent into hell was really a victory march. He went into the stronghold of Satan and his demons and announced to them that He had decisively defeated them. His dying on the cross was a master stroke of victory because it meant that He had saved His people and had vanquished the great foe of mankind.

c. *The Second Probationists:* Hell is to be understood as the abode of those who have died having rejected the gospel. Now Christ goes to them again, making them a second offer and giving them one more opportunity to repent. They appeal to I Peter 3:19-20; 4:6.

25 How Long Was Jesus' Body in the Tomb?

Q. *How long did Jesus' dead body repose in the tomb?*

A. It is quite difficult from the references to the Passover and the Preparation in Mark 15, Luke 23, and John 19 to spell out the specific time data here. We are dependent upon such reputable Jewish Christian Biblical scholars as Edersheim for our judgments. He maintains that in general the Jewish people (with the exception of the Sadducees who celebrated it on Friday) observed that annual historic feast on Thursday. That would leave 6 P.M. on Friday night to early Sunday morning as the time span for the reposing of Jesus' body in the grave.

But what about Jesus' prediction in Matthew 12:40 to the effect that even as Jonah spent three days and three nights in the interior of the mammoth fish, so too He would repose for three days and three nights in the heart of the earth?

Apparently He was not speaking in technical scientific terms. As John Calvin says: "This is in accordance with a well-known figure of speech (synecdoche). As the night is an appendage of the day, or rather, as the day consists of two parts, light and darkness, he expresses a day by a day and a night, and when there was a half a day, he puts down a whole day." Lightfoot, the English scholar, says the same when citing parallel passages (I Sam. 30:12, 13; Hos. 6:2; etc.) and quotes the Jewish Talmud to the effect that in the Jewish use of the words *day* and *night* "any part of such a period is counted as the whole."

We are to assume then, if Calvin and Lightfoot are correct, that the intention of Jesus (Matt. 12:90) was not scientific exactitude of the time span that His body should lie in the tomb.

Q. *Did Jesus' resurrected body have to change into a spiritual body when He ascended into heaven?*

A. Nothing in Scripture bears this out.

In the Lucan passage (Luke 24:39) the Lord is concerned about emphasizing the reality of His resurrection body. His disciples were tempted at first, so it seems, to regard His appearance after His resurrection as an apparition. And in order to convince them that He had actually arisen in the flesh, Jesus invited them to touch Him.

In the great resurrection chapter (I Cor. 15), the Apostle Paul is concerned to teach that our resurrected, glorified body will not be identical in all respects with this physical organism that we now possess. A change will ensue, but nonetheless it will be a substantial, physical body that we will receive. Christ speaks of *flesh and bones* in Luke 24 rather than of *flesh and blood,* and it may be, as Dean Alford maintains, that the former will be the nature of our resurrection bodies.

Incidentally, in his comment on the Luke 24 passage, Calvin suggests that the marks of the nails in the hands and feet of Jesus and the mark of the sword thrust in His side *continued only for a time.* This, of course, is speculative.

Questions

1. When Jesus said on the cross "It is finished" did He

89

mean that this marked the end of His humiliation because of sin? And yet, was not His burial a continuation of that humiliation?

2. Is burial one of the penalties of sin? (See Gen. 3:19.)

3. Since some people have been buried although they were still alive, how can the burial of Jesus be said to be a proof of His death?

4. Our bodies begin to decompose soon after death. Apparently that was not the case with Jesus (Ps. 16:10; Acts 2:27, 31; 13:35, 37). Is not this bodily decay one of the elements in the punishment for sin? Why then was Jesus exempted from this bodily deterioration?

5. Are our burial ceremonies and rites (funerals, etc.) Christian? Or do they have elements of paganism intertwined? If so, how can we purge them of these pagan elements?

6. In what sense did Jesus sanctify the grave for the believer?

7. Did Joseph of Arimathea take care of Jesus' burial and provide a tomb for Him because he was a social activist or because he was a follower of Christ?

8. In what sense is Christ called the "firstfruits" in the great resurrection chapter (I Cor. 15)? Is this related to one of the religious feasts of the Jews in the Old Testament?

9. Christ is also called "the firstborn from the dead" (I Cor. 15:20; Col. 1:18). Since others (Lazarus, the son of widow of Nain, etc.) had been raised before He was, how can this be said of Him? Does the word *first* refer to position or to point in time?

10. How would you disprove from the Scriptures the following denials of the truth of Christ's resurrection: *Fraud* theory: it was a falsehood perpetrated by His disciples. They spread the false news of His rising from the dead; the *Swoon* theory: Jesus never really died but only went into a coma; the *Visionary* theory: the people were disturbed in mind and highly excited, supposing that they saw Jesus but actually never did; and the *Mythical* theory: this is a story

from pagan sources that was later on incorporated into the Bible?

11. Of what practical significance for us is the resurrection of Christ (Rom. 1:5; 5:10; I Cor. 15:22) and the ascension of Christ (John 14:2; 17:24; Heb. 9:11, 12)?

12. What is the ascended Christ doing today (John 5:26; 16:13; Rom. 8:34; Eph. 1:20)? In what sense is He the Lord of history?

26 Did Christ Die for Apostate Leaders?

Q. *Were the false teachers mentioned in II Peter 2:1 (those who bring destructive heresies into the church) bought and ransomed by Christ?*

A. This text is difficult to understand and interpret.

One commentator says: "though Christ may be denied in various ways, yet Peter, *as I think,* refers here to what is expressed by Jude, that is, when the grace of God is turned into lasciviousness; for Christ redeemed us, that He might have a people separated from all the pollutions of the world and devoted to holiness and innocency. They, then, who throw off the bridle and give themselves up to all kinds of licentiousness, are not unjustly said to deny Christ, by whom they have been redeemed. Hence, that the doctrine of the Gospel may remain whole and complete among us, let this be fixed in our minds, that we have been redeemed by Christ, that He may be the Lord of our life and of our death, and that our main object ought to be to live to Him and to die in Him" (Calvin).

Calvin subscribed to the doctrine of particular atonement (Christ died for the elect), but since he could not reconcile that truth with its apparent contradiction in this passage, he bypassed the problem and drew from it a practical admonition that those redeemed by Christ must live for Him. And to this, of course, we all agree.

The problem remains, however. How are these words

to be understood in the light of the truth of particular atonement?

It is suggested by another commentator that these words apply to the substance of the denial of the false teachers. What did these apostate leaders teach? They taught that Christ did not die for men. They denied His divinity and His expiatory sacrifice. Their doctrine was false precisely because it was a denial of the sub-stitutionary atonement of Christ. This interpretation is appealing, but it is a manipulation of the text. Peter says specifically: "denying . . . the Master *that bought them.*"

D. H. Kromminga, a profound scholar and devout Christian, one who also subscribed to the truth of par-ticular atonement, in 1942 wrote a series of articles on "The Scope of the Atonement." After marshaling the Biblical evidence and noting that Scripture teaches that Christ "bought" the Ephesian church (Acts 20:28), the redeemed in glory (Rev. 5:9), and the apostate teachers (II Peter 2:1), he asserted that a distinction must be made. Christ did not "buy" all of these parties men-tioned in the same sense. These false prophets and teachers apparently were not heirs of glory, but since they belonged historically and legally to God's people, there is a sense, so he maintained, in which Christ died for them. Professor Kromminga went on to say that the sincere and unfeigned offer of the gospel must be un-derstood in this context. That offer is inextricably tied up with Christ's atonement. "If He had not brought a sacrifice sufficient to atone for and expiate the sins of the whole world, it (the offer) could not be sincerely made." And when the offer is refused, the rejecter ag-gravates his guilt and crucifies the Son of God afresh (see *The Banner,* July 24, 1942, pp. 669 ff.).

Questions

1. A principle of Bible interpretation is to the effect that

the more clear passages of Scripture are to be given the preference. With this in mind, analyze the present problem in the light of such passages as Matthew 1:21; John 10:11, 15; and others.

2. Romans 5:18 ("the free gift came unto *all men* to justification of life") is frequently cited to prove that Christ purchased all men by His blood. Does this text prove the point? (Consult the context [vss. 12-17] to see what the basic teaching is here.)

3. Christ said, "If ye love me, keep my commandments" (John 14:15). Not one of us keeps the commandments of Christ perfectly. Does this imply that we deny Him upon occasion? If it does, and we are regenerated persons, can it not be said that deniers of Christ are bought by Him?

4. Sometimes we use the word *buy* in a figurative way. When we accept the view or option expressed by someone else we say: "I'll buy that." Is it possible that in II Peter 2:1 the word is used figuratively?

5. The covenant can be understood in a narrower and in a wider sense. In the narrower sense it includes only the elect, those who will inherit the glories of heaven. In the broader sense it includes the Christian community comprising families in which at least one of the parents is a confessing Christian. Could we say that Christ died for that broader convenantal community? (See Acts 20:28-31.)

6. How do the Canons of Dort use the word *bought* in connection with the redemption of Christ (II, 8)? (Bear in mind that this is a theological work and it may use the word in a different sense than do the Scriptures.)

CUSTOMS AND PRACTICES
OF THE EARLY CHURCH

Should Christians Fast? **27**

Q. *In view of Jesus' answer to His disciples as recorded in Matthew 9:15, is it demanded of Christians to fast?*

A. In the Old Testament with all of its regulations there was but one fast day prescribed for the Israelites. It was the annual Day of Atonement when the high priest made expiation for the sins of the nation (Lev. 16:29, 31). Fasting here is described as an "afflicting of the soul."

Other fastings mentioned in the Old Testament were of a voluntary nature. They were designed to demonstrate deep grief at loss by death (e.g., David's mourning for Saul, II Sam. 1:12, 13; and for Abner, II Sam. 3:35); personal disappointments (e.g., Hannah's childlessness, I Sam. 1:7); sadness because of the state of the nation (e.g., Nehemiah over Jerusalem, Neh. 1:4); and to indicate a great crisis or crucial event (e.g., Moses at the receiving of the law on Sinai, Exod. 34:28).

Usually the fast period was of one day duration with total abstinence of food or taking a meal late in the day; in exceptional instances it was extended to three days (e.g., when the Jews were threatened with extinction, Esther 4:16) and even to seven (e.g., when the citizens of Jabesh-Gilead had recovered and buried the body of Saul, I Sam. 31:13). It appears that fasting as a barren, formal ritual became a real danger for Israel in the later years of the monarchy, and hence some of the prophets warn against its abuse (Isa. 58:4ff.; Zech. 7:5-6; etc.).

When Jesus engaged in His public ministry He did not condemn fasting, as the quotation at the head of this article indicates. On the contrary, He implied that it was a fitting and commendable religious exercise. He did rebuke the Pharisees for making a show of it and parading their piety (Matt. 6:16-18), but He did not condemn the practice because of its abuse.

In the apostolic church there seems to have been no definite custom in this regard. It was not regularly practiced. We do find a few references to it. For instance, when the first foreign missionaries were sent out from Antioch (Acts 13:2-3) it was preceded by prayer and fasting. Exceptional circumstances impelled the early church to engage in it. But it was never presented as mandatory; and Paul in his great chapter on adiaphora, or things indifferent, clearly implies that this is one of those matters on which a Christian may not bind the conscience of another (Rom. 14:6).

As soon as we get out of the apostolic church period the situation changes, however. By A.D. 300 fasting had become compulsory and had found a place in the regulated life of the church member. Gradually there developed in Roman Catholicism four great fast seasons, of which Lent is the most extensive and best known.

The Reformers had no fault to find with the practice as such, but warned against the superstition and ritualistic ceremonialism that had attached itself to it. The Westminster Confession reflects their attitude when it states that "solemn fastings are in their times and seasons to be used in a holy and religious manner."

In the history of our own nation it was practiced in New England days. The Plymouth colony held a day of fasting on July 16, 1623, because of prolonged drought, and the Massachussetts Bay colony called one on January 19, 1637, when a doctrinal controversy, Antinomianism, threatened to disrupt the colony.

It is quite evident from the foregoing, that fasting has something to commend it. It may serve as an aid in our religious exercise. All of us know from experience that a heavy meal tends to make one drowsy and sluggish. It is hardly conducive to mental or spiritual alertness and concentration. Conversely, eating sparingly lends greater powers of concentration to one who is focusing his heart and mind upon God.

It is well to bear in mind, however, that this is one of the optional phases of Christian practice. You may engage in it, you may find it helpful so to do upon occasion, but you are not obligated so to do. Some acts of worship are expressly required. Prayer is one of them. Other acts are accessory, and fasting is one of them.

But even though we may not choose to fast in the technical sense of the word we should certainly respect its underlying purpose, namely that we eat temperately prior to religious exercises so that without digestive distraction we may be able to concentrate upon the things of God.

Questions

1. Why did Jesus fast prior to His first great temptation (Matt. 4)?

2. Comment on this statement: "The theory which placed the origin and seat of sin in the *body* tended to give value to the practice of fasting." Why should this be the case?

3. Since in our affluent society we tend to overeat and overindulge our appetites and become victims of diseases that are traceable to our refined foods, would it not be good for Christians to fast and thus exercise stewardship over their bodies?

4. What do you think of the argument of Clement of

Alexandria (Stromata, XIII) who had little use for fasting and said: "Paul declares that the Kingdom of Heaven consists not in food and drink, neither therefore in abstaining from wine and flesh, 'but in righteousness, peace and joy in the Holy Spirit'" (Rom. 14:17)?

5. The early church did fast upon occasion (Acts 13:2; 14:23; II Cor. 6:5). We rarely if ever do. Granted that it is optional on our part, how can we encourage it? Would the day of Prayer for Peace be an appropriate occasion? How would you react if your church called for a day of fasting and prayer?

6. Calvin wrote: "Holy and legitimate fasting is directed to three ends, for we practice it either as a restraint on the flesh, to preserve it from licentiousness; or as a preparation for prayers or pious meditations; or as a testing of our humiliation in the presence of God, when we are desirous of confessing our guilt before Him" (*Inst.* IV, 12, 15-20). Are his views borne out by Biblical examples?

Should We Practice Footwashing? **28**

Q. *Does footwashing belong with our communion celebration?*

A. There are some who claim that it does.

C. E. Bowen in *The Lord's Supper and Feet Washing* writes, "If Jesus had not intended to connect them together, He would have given the Supper apart from feet washing" (p. 83), and, since "Jesus instituted this Supper and feet washing, no one has the right to contradict its validity. For this reason we are safe in saying that it is as much in force today as when Jesus instituted it" (p. 109).

The Biblical setting of this question is John 13:4-5 where we read that Jesus "riseth from supper, and layeth aside his garments; and he took a towel, and girded himself. Then he poureth water into the basin, and began to wash the disciple's feet, and to wipe them with the towel wherewith he was girded." Then follows Peter's expostulations and Jesus' reference to His betrayer.

The washing of feet was a social custom and practice in New Testament Palestine.

Open sandals were common footwear and the streets were dusty and muddy; consequently a basin of water was standing at the door of every home and the entrant either washed his own feet or a servant performed those ablutions for him.

But that social custom is not in operation here. This washing was not done upon entering the dwelling where the Supper was instituted. It took place later, either during the meal or after the Supper was finished.

Is it an intrinsic part of the communion celebration? Neither Matthew (26:26ff.), nor Mark (14:22ff.), nor Luke (22:19ff.) mention it in their accounts of the institution of the Supper. Neither does Paul in I Corinthians 11 where he declares that he is passing on to the church that which he "received of the Lord" (vs. 23).

It would seem, then, that this foot washing is symbolical in character and that the Lord was teaching His disciples the lessons of humble service and esteem for one another.

Incidentally, we need to be careful with the demand that we duplicate the first Lord's Supper in every respect. That first one was held at night, in an upper room, after a regular meal, and with only men present. There are incidentals which we can regard as passing in significance. We must insist on retaining the heart of the institution.

Questions

1. If footwashing was not an integral part of the original communion celebration but rather one of its "accidents," what essentials of that original celebration must be retained?

2. In that warm Oriental climate the danger of leprosy was always present. Cleanliness of body was one of the safeguards against it. And since leprosy often began in the extremities (feet and fingers) is it likely that this was a sanitary measure pertinent to those days? Since we have our own measures of sanitation and hygienic devices, is it likely that this practice has been replaced?

3. Looking at the practice from a different angle, we note from the Scriptures (Gen. 18:4; 19:2; Judg. 19:21)

that footwashing, necessary in that day because of the dusty roads and because sandals were worn, was one of the rites of hospitality. You showed your friendliness and hospitableness by providing your guest with a basin of water and a towel. That was one of the mores of that day. But since times have changed, has this practice also gone by the board?

4. What significance do you read into the anointing of the feet of Jesus by the tears of the penitent woman (Luke 7:44)?

5. How do you react to these views expressed by Martin Luther: "We have nothing to do with feet-washing with water, otherwise it is not only the feet of the twelve, but those of everybody we should wash. People will be much more benefited if a general bath were at once ordered, and the whole body washed. If you wish to wash your neighbor's feet, see that your heart is really humble, and help everyone in being better."

29 Is Anointment by Oil an Ordained Christian Practice?

Q. *In the light of James 5:14 and of Mark 6:13, should we anoint the sick with oil?*

A. There are three interpretations given to these verses. We may call them the sacramental, the medicinal, and the confirmatory.

1. *The Roman Catholic Church has drawn on these words to deduce from them its seventh sacrament.* It is called Extreme Unction and it is admitted to one who is dying. A priest will administer it, for example, to one fatally injured and pinned under a wreck. Its earliest usage in this way (as the final Sacrament) was in the eighth century. At that point in history it was no longer given to one on his sickbed but as remission of sins to one who was on his deathbed. It was a most radical departure from the original rendering of James and Mark, and yet the Council of Trent in 1549 did not hesitate to affirm it a sacrament "implied by Mark and promulgated by James the apostle and brother of the Lord." But this is a gross misuse of the Biblical references. Farrar was quite right in saying about James 5:14-15, "Neither for Extreme Unction, nor for sacramental confession, nor for sacerdotal absolution, nor for fanatical extravagance does this passage afford the slighest sanction."

2. *A second possible interpretation is that the oil in this instance was medicinally applied.* Isaiah in his prophecy speaks about wounds and says of them that "they have not been closed, nor bound up, nor

mollified with oil" (Isa. 1:6). And in the parable of the Good Samaritan the victim of the brigands had his wounds bandaged and treated with oil and wine (Luke 10:34). In the Middle East, olive oil is still used for that purpose, much in the same way that our nurses render bodily comfort by rubbing alcohol. The reason then why oil is mentioned in this instance is that after making the patient more comfortable it is possible to have more meaningful prayer. If the patient is uncomfortable and sore, he tends to be introvertive and has great difficulty in concentrating his attention upon God in the prayer of intercession that is offered in his behalf. With the measure of comfort that the oil gives to him physically, prayer can mean much more to him. It is well to note in this regard that James states that the "prayer of faith [not the oil] shall save him that is sick." This medicinal interpretation is very plausible.

3. *So does the third alternative, namely, that this was something in the nature of a confirmatory ceremony.* Then it must be viewed in the light of the temporary gift of healing possessed by the disciples in the early church. The Gospels mention miracles performed by the disciples of Jesus. So does the Book of Acts. Furthermore, oil in the Scriptural record frequently represents the Holy Spirit. And it was the Holy Spirit who enabled the disciples to perform miracles. How fitting then that the accompanying oil would indicate that fact. This ability to perform miracles lasted only until the last book of the Bible was written. Then it terminated. And if this oil is to confirm that gift and show the source of this miraculous power, its administration would terminate too at this point. This third alternative is suggested by Calvin and it too has much to commend it.

QUESTIONS

1. The Roman Catholics include Extreme Unction among

the sacraments. On what basis do we limit the sacraments to two: Baptism and the Lord's Supper?

2. Compare the definition of a sacrament by a modern theologian, Paul Tillich, with that of John Calvin. Says Tillich, "The whole universe is sacramental. . . . A sacrament is any object or event in which the transcendent is perceived to be present." According to John Calvin, "A sacrament is an external symbol by which God seals the promise of His goodwill towards us, in order to strengthen the weakness of our faith; and we, in turn, testify before Him . . . our devotion to His service."

3. The ancients used oil very commonly for medicinal purposes. For example, Pliny said that olive oil was good to warm the body and fortify it against cold. Tertullian, a second century Christian lawyer, cites an instance of a cure from disease by using oil. James 5:14 may reflect this practice. If so, it is what is called a "time-conditioned" practice. How can we determine which of these things in the Biblical record are "time-conditioned" and which are permanent and timeless? Does a knowledge of the times in which the Bible was written help one here?

4. The editor of the religious periodical, *Plain Truth,* in writing about his daughter who had been advised by her doctor to have an internal cyst removed by surgery and who had been anointed with oil by her father in accord with James 5:14, wrote: "I advised her (because she hardly knew whether to rely on surgery or on the anointment by oil) to rely on whichever method she had the most faith. If she had more faith in the doctor and in surgery than in God and in His written promises, then undergo the operation without delay." Was that good advice on the part of a parent to his child?

5. Using a concordance, look up the various Bible passages in which *oil* is mentioned. Note particularly these passages in which it is connected with the operation of the Holy Spirit. Does this give some clue as to its Biblical usage?

Did the Gift of Tongues Cease? **30**

Q. *Was the speaking in tongues limited to the early church?*

A. Before we examine the Biblical data on the subject, let me say that the "gift of tongues" is understood and interpreted in at least two ways. It may mean the ability given by the Spirit to an individual, enabling him to speak a foreign language without going through the trouble of mastering it first. Or it may mean the power to speak a lofty, unknown language of the soul, made intelligible only to the person involved by supernatural interpretation.

Now we turn to the pertinent Bible passages.

The first reference to the gift of tongues is in Mark 16:17 where the Lord is recorded as saying in His farewell, "And these signs shall accompany them that believe; in my name ... they shall speak with new tongues. ... The key word here is *sign*. The gift of tongues and the gift of healing are confirmations or proofs that the truth Jesus' followers proclaimed had divine power and sanction and proceeded from God.

The first fulfillment of this prophecy was on the day of Pentecost when the Spirit was poured out and the disciples "began to speak with other tongues, as the Spirit gave them utterance" (Acts 2:4). The second fulfillment occurred in the home of Cornelius the centurion who was converted to Christ. The Spirit descended upon this new band of disciples, and "they heard them speak with tongues and magnify God" (Acts 10:46). The third fulfillment was at Ephesus where we read that as "the Holy Spirit came on them; they spake with tongues, and prophesied" (Acts 19:6). In all of these instances the gift of tongues was designed to prove to others that the spiritual change these converts had undergone in response to the gospel was induced by God.

The last Biblical reference to the "gift of tongues" occurs in Paul's letter to the Corinthians. That church was marred by a contentious spirit as well as by shameful disorders and immoral practices. Paul's aim in writing them is to instruct, reprove, and reform. Among the evils that marked the church was the coveting of such spiritual gifts that would inflate the ego of the possessor and attract the admiration of others. It appears that the "gift of tongues" was especially coveted.

Paul rebukes the Corinthians on two counts. They were forgetting that this gift was intended to be a *sign* (I Cor. 14:22; cf. Mark 16:17) and that the primary aim was the edification of the church. The gift was being grossly abused. Members in the church were desirous of possessing it only in order that they might excite the wonder of others and build up their own self-esteem.

Quite obviously this gift was soon withdrawn. The missionaries apparently did not possess such a labor-saving device whereby they could cross the language barriers without any effort on their part. Paul and Barnabas surely did not understand the language of Lycaonia (Acts 14:1-18) for, if they had, they would have protested much earlier the preparations being made to honor them as gods.

So we conclude that this gift was for a limited time only. It was not intended to be a permanent bequest.

It was adapted to the first proclamation of the gospel and the setting up of the Christian church. When the church was just getting under way, this was designed to be a *sign* or a proof of the power and presence of the true and living God.

QUESTIONS

1. Pentecost (Acts 2) has sometimes been called the counterpart of Babel (Gen. 11). How are these two events related in God's plan?

2. Why was Pentecost so significant as far as missions was concerned? Augustine said that each one of the disciples could speak all of the different languages represented there. Chrysostom, another early church father, said that each disciple could speak one foreign language and that indicated the area to which he was assigned. What do you think? Did they retain this ability to speak foreign languages all their lifetime?

3. Jesus told His disciples that in the future they need take no thought of what they should speak since the Spirit would speak in them (Matt. 10:19, 20; Mark 13:11; 16:17). Do you think He was predicting this speaking in tongues that occurred on Pentecost and thereafter? If not, what did He have in mind?

4. In I Corinthians 12:8-31 and I Corinthians 14 Paul classifies the spiritual gifts of the church. How does the speaking in tongues rate in this classification? Does this indicate its relative importance?

5. There are those who distinguish between *baptism of the Spirit* and *born again of the Spirit*. The latter are second class Christians while the former are first class Christians because, in addition to being born again, they are baptized by the Spirit, proof of which is to be found in the fact that they can speak in tongues. Do the following Scripture passages support such a distinction? John 3:3, 5; Acts 2:3, 4; Gal. 5:16; Titus 3:5.

6. In Romans 14 Paul speaks about *adiaphora* or things

indifferent. A case in point is whether or not a Christian may eat meat that has been offered to idols. He calls that a thing indifferent. Does speaking in tongues fall into this class?

7. If one of your fellow church members claimed to be able to speak in tongues, how would you react?

8. Give your evaluation of this judgment of the gift of tongues in the early church: "This subject is not merely curious and interesting, but full of practical moment. For one thing, it shows how well the Gospel message was accredited in its first promulgation. It fixes attention on the high consequence of preaching the Gospel; of declaring its message with a glowing, burning earnestness, and of obtaining the live coal which is to kindle the heart from off God's altar. For another, we learn from the apostle [Paul] that faith, hope, and charity were better than this physical endowment, as having a more abiding character."

Was Pentecost Repeated? **31**

Q. *Can we speak of more than one outpouring of the Holy Spirit in the history of the church?*

A. There is but one Pentecost. It is a unique event that will never be repeated. It occurred once for all.

First of all, the classic passage in Joel (2:28-32) contains no hint of a series of Pentecosts or sporadic outpourings from time to time. There is one climactic event towards which the Old Testament is heading.

Furthermore, Jesus speaks in that pattern of thought. So John interprets His words to the Pharisees when Jesus referred to the "rivers of living water" that will flow. That, says John, applies to *the* giving of the Spirit after our Lord's ascension (John 7:39). Jesus Himself promised the Comforter who would not come and go but remain with them forever (John 14:16). Consequently, Paul does not hesitate to call us temples or homes of the Spirit in which He dwells (I Cor. 3:16; etc.). This is one great opening of the sluice gates which is not inappropriately called the "birthday" of the Christian church. And, like a birthday in our frame of reference, it may be commemorated but not actually repeated.

But, it will be argued, What then about those "later outpourings" recorded in the book of Acts (8:15-17; 10:44-48; 19:1-6)? If you will check these passages, you will note that, in all cases, they concern Gentiles.

The initial event concerned only Jews and proselytes (those converted to the Jewish religion). The others, then, must be interpreted to be an extension of that initial outpouring. This is the other side of the coin. Not only Jews are to be recipients; so too the Gentiles. The church now enters upon a new period in her history. She is now the universal church, given the Spirit, and duty bound to go out and witness to the world.

QUESTIONS

1. What was the significance of each of the three signs on Pentecost (Acts 2)?

2. What various functions does the Holy Spirit, the Third Person of the Trinity, perform? (See Gen. 1:3; Exod. 28:3, 6; I Sam. 11;6; Ps. 104:30; II Peter 1:21; etc.)

3. How is the work of the Holy Spirit in the Old Testament dispensation to be distinguished from His work in the New Testament age? Is it merely a matter of quantity?

4. What work does the Spirit do in connection with redemption and in connection with the formation and development of the Christian church?

5. In Acts 10:44 we read that the Holy Spirit fell on those who heard the Word of God. Does that same phenomenon occur today with the preaching of the gospel?

6. Paul urges his readers to "be filled with the Spirit" (Eph. 5:18). How can we carry out this command?

7. Occasionally we hear radio evangelists pray for "another Pentecost." Is this a proper prayer to make?

8. What does it mean to "walk by the Spirit" (Gal. 5:16)? Does the context give you a clue as to its practical implication?

9. According to I Samuel 16:14a "the Spirit of Jehovah departed from Saul." Is it possible to lose the Spirit once you have it? Or does this verse refer to some work of the Spirit other than that of regeneration?

Is Faith Healing Real? **32**

Q. *Are faith healings real or fraudulent?*

A. There are some false assumptions and there is some bad theology in many of the purported "faith healings" of our day.

Evangelists, such as Oral Roberts, assume that since Christ came to save the whole man, a sound body is as possible here on earth as a fruit of the atonement as is a sound soul. He fails to reckon with the fact that even as our souls retain something of the vestiges of sin, so too the physical implications of sin are not obliterated when one becomes a Christian. He assumes too that restoration from illness and disease is directly proportionate to the amount of faith a person has. Adequate faith will cure anyone of anything. Conversely, failure to be healed is but an indication of weakness of faith.

But that assumption is invalid. Undoubtedly the Apostle Paul had as virile a faith as anyone. Despite it he obviously kept his "thorn in the flesh" to his dying day. Roberts and his colleagues assume that bodily health is life's greatest blessing and one of life's highest aims. The Scriptures never speak in those terms. They constantly emphasize that submission to the will of God has the highest priority. We are not to pray for the healing of another *because* it is God's will, as some "faith healers" assume, but *if* it is His will. We are warned through Isaiah: "My thoughts are not your thoughts, neither are your ways my ways, said Jehovah. For as the heavens are higher than the earth, so are my ways higher than your ways, and my thoughts than your thoughts" (Isa. 55:8, 9).

Our recourse is to be that of Paul who heard God saying to him: "My grace is sufficient for thee." It is assumed too that there are some who are especially called by God to draw out latent faith so as to be healed. We insist that a "call" to some phase of religious work be authenticated by an official religious body.

But now to return to the question: What about "faith healing"?

The term itself is a misnomer. Faith does not heal. It has no inherent curative properties. It is God who heals, and the God who heals is the Lord.

And since God is the Lord of life and death, He determines how and if a man is to be cured if illness or disease strikes him down.

In grace He has provided physicians, medications, and advancements in medical science, and by those means a great many illnesses and sicknesses are counteracted and cured. In our use of them we make grateful use of one of the benefactions of God.

There are instances too when the medical profession acknowledges itself to be at the end of its medical tether as far as remedies are concerned and pronounces the case to be a terminal one, whereupon restoration ensues in answer to fervent prayer. This does not necessarily mean that the physician erred in his prognosis. It means that prayer is efficacious and it means that God is sovereign. He is not limited to the natural means that He has given. When He chooses to supersede them He does so. Nor is such restoration an indication of great and robust faith. There are chronic invalids whose faith in God's goodness and love is unshaken and yet whose disability is not removed. Nor is such a cure due to the superior technique of a practitioner. It is simply the gracious act of a sovereign God who has determined to give healing in this instance.

Questions

1. Miracles were performed by the apostles in the early church (Acts 3:7-8; 14:9-10; etc.). Why was this the case?

2. Comment on the definition of miracles by H. Wade, namely: "Extraordinary acts of God, transcending the ordinary processes of nature, wrought in connection with the end of revelation" (*International Standard Bible Encyclopedia*) and John Calvin's judgment: "It is unreasonable to ask miracles or to find them where there is no new gospel" (*Inst.* I, 26).

3. Sometimes a person who has a terminal disease and is given but a few months to live, recovers and lives a normal life again. He and his family may and often do call it a "miracle." Is that judgment correct? If it is, is such sudden miraculous help more wonderful than recovery by using the ordinary medical means?

4. May a Christian, who has tried all available medical means without success, seek the help of a "faith healer"?

5. James 5:15 is often appealed to in proof of the fact that faith heals. Is that what the verse teaches?

6. What is the church's duty and responsibility towards those who are physically ill?

7. Is it good logic to argue that since sickness and illness are due to sin, when sin is forgiven the illness or sickness ought to be removed?

8. Comment on this excerpt from the biography by D. Taplinger in which he quotes Oral Roberts as saying: "I believe that God is a good God. A good God cannot want His children to be sick in spirit, mind and body. A good God wants His children to be happy, healthy and prosperous. A good God detests sickness and misery. Therefore, it is only when people do not believe that God is a good God that sickness and misery befall them."

Note: It might be well for one of the members to report on such a work as Warfield's *Miracles Yesterday and Today*. It gives some interesting insights.

THE END TIME

Is Death a State of Unconsciousness?

Q. *In what state are we between death and judgment day — conscious or unconscious? If conscious, will we recognize one another?*

A. It is very true that death is sometimes compared with sleep in the Scriptures (Matt. 9:24; Acts 7:60; I Cor. 15:51; etc.). That figure of speech is used presumably to point out that there is a break between these two phases of existence (even as in sleep we are detached from the activities of the world), and that a rest is involved. It does not mean a state of unconsciousness however. Immediately after death the believer enters upon conscious communion with God and those who have gone on before.

As the Westminster Confession puts it: "The souls of the righteous, being then made perfect in holiness, are received into the highest heavens, where they behold the face of God in light and glory, waiting for the full redemption of their bodies."

Many texts imply that conscious existence. A few will suffice. The Lord tells the penitent thief on the cross, "Today shalt thou be with me in Paradise" (Luke 23:43). When Stephen dies as a martyr he anticipates immediate communion with his Savior when he prays, "Lord Jesus, receive my spirit" (Acts 7:59); Paul expresses his deep desire to depart and "be with Christ" (Phil. 1:23); and the book of Revelation describes the souls of the martyrs under the altar pleading for the speedy judgment of God (Rev. 6:9-11) and the redeemed singing praises about the throne of God (Rev. 7:9-10).

Now as to the second part of the question. Scriptural data is scanty but recognition of others is implied in the fact that the disciples recognized Jesus after His resurrection; in the Lord's teaching that many "will sit down with Abraham, Isaac, and Jacob in the kingdom of heaven" (Matt. 8:11) holding conversation with them; in the story of the Rich Man and Lazarus (Luke 16:19ff) where there is mutual recognition in the next world; and in Paul's confident anticipation that when the Lord comes again, the Thessalonian Christians will be his joy (1 Thess. 2:19). We are limited to inference here but it is sufficiently strong to indicate that recognition of each other is a carry-over phenomenon to the next world.

QUESTIONS

1. Those who teach a "soul sleep" after death appeal to such passages as Matthew 9:24; I Corinthians 15:6; and I Thessalonians 4:13. How must these verses be interpreted?

2. When death for disobedience was threatened in Genesis 2:17, was this a reference to physical or spiritual death?

3. Is death a punishment as far as the believer is concerned? If so, how do you understand the truth that Christ bore the punishment of sin for us? Is death a punishment for the unbeliever?

4. Submitting to anesthesia in an operation is sometimes advanced as an analogy of what occurs when a person dies. Just as a patient under anesthesia is unaware of the passage of time and seems to be living in the eternally present, so too is the experience of the person between death and resurrection. What do you think of this analogy?

5. What does Luke 16:19-31 teach about the state of

the soul after death? What, in your estimation, is the main teaching of this parable?

6. The writer of the Hebrews, in speaking of the departed, says that "we are surrounded with a great cloud of witnesses" (Heb. 12:1, RSV). Does he mean to say that those who have gone before are like spectators in the arena, watching us who are still playing on the field of life? Are they aware of what is going on here below?

7. How much sorrow is legitimate at the death of a Christian?

8. Comment on the quotation: "Man is mortal and death is not the wages of sin but the debt of nature."

34 Must the Christian Still Be Judged?

Q. *Will the Christian also be judged on the Final Judgment Day?*

A. Such passages as II Corinthians 5:10 and Revelation 20:13 clearly indicate that Christians, as well as unbelievers will be judged.

But that must be rightly understood. It does not mean that a person's eternal destiny will be determined on that final day. That is set when he dies. One who dies in Christ has already been adjudged to be an heir of God throughout all eternity, and one who dies without Christ faces certain condemnation.

Judgment Day serves two main purposes. One is to publicly declare the eternal destinies.

The other is to determine status in eternity. Abundance of good works in the Christian life on earth means greater gracious rewards in the next life. Paul writes that "he that soweth sparingly shall reap also sparingly; and he that soweth bountifully shall reap also bountifully" (II Cor. 9:6). And the same diversity appears to be true of the state of the lost. You must remember that our Lord said to the Palestinian cities that heard the gospel and rejected it, "It shall be more tolerable for Tyre and Sidon in that day of judgment, than for you" (Matt. 11:22).

"Wherefore, my beloved brethen, be ye stedfast, unmovable, *always abounding* in the work of the Lord, forasmuch as ye know that your labor is not vain in the Lord" (I Cor. 15:58) (italics added).

Q. *Is the Final Judgment public or private?*

A. In the Biblical passages that deal with the final judgment, at least two things are stressed.

One is the inevitability of judgment for every man. No one will be exempt. No one can escape apprehension by the Judge of the world. Paul writes that "we must all be made manifest before the judgment-seat of Christ; that each one may receive the things done in the body, according to what he hath done, whether it be good or bad" (II Cor. 5:10).

The other is the recall and disclosure of the life history of each man. The exposure is thorough and detailed. When the books are opened, "the dead are judged ... according to their works" (Rev. 20:12). It appears that every nook and cranny will be laid bare. But whether this revelation will be made to others we do not know. Whether *others* will be apprised of the specific nature of *our* misdoing, we have no means of knowing. I would think that if it was a sin involving others or against others, those directly involved would be included in the trial scene. But it seems to me that the Scripture is silent on this point. The main intent of the Bible is to urge us to repentance when we sin; to assure us that we do have an Advocate with the Father in the person of our Savior; and that if our sins are forgiven in Him we need not fear the Great Assize at the end of days.

Q. *According to II Corinthians 5:10 we will be judged according to our works. In what sense is that true?*

A. There is a twofold sense in which this is true.

One is the fact that works constitute the touchstone or the barometer of faith. As James pointed out so graphically, faith shows itself through works. An intellectual, abstract, theoretical faith is one that belies the name. True faith must evidence itself. The life one lives and the deeds one performs in service to God and fellow man are the concrete exhibition of faith. And when those works are judged and evaluated, so too is the underlying faith.

The other is the fact that our works here determine our status in eternity. Abundance of good works in the Christian life below means greater gracious rewards in the next life. Paul writes that "he that soweth sparingly shall reap also sparingly; and he that soweth bountifully shall reap also bountifully" (II Cor. 9:6). And the same diversity appears to be true of the state of the lost. Didn't our Lord say to the Palestinian cities that had the gospel opportunity and rejected it, "It shall be *more tolerable* for Tyre and Sidon in the day of judgment, than for you" (Matt. 11:22) (italics added)? Yes.

Questions

1. The Final Judgment is called in the Scriptures "that day" (Matt. 7:22) and the "day of wrath" (Rom. 2:5). How do you answer the objection that it would be impossible to hold court on one day for the millions who must appear before God? Or is this to be a lengthy process?

2. Since a Christian's destiny is already set at death but he does not enter upon his inheritance until the Great Judgment Day, the analogy has been drawn to that of the president of the United States who is elected to his office in November but does not become president until January. Is that a valid analogy?

3. What comfort for the Christian is to be found in the fact that Christ is to serve as Judge on that day?

4. There are some Christian groups that hold to several future judgments. They do so on the basis of the following texts: Matthew 7:22, 23; 25:31-46; John 5:28, 29; Acts

17:31; II Peter 3:7; Revelation 11:18; 20:11-15. How do you interpret these passages?

5. On the basis of such passages from the Word of God as Matthew 11:21-24; 25:31-46; Romans 2:12-16, what standards will be used on the Judgment Day?

6. Schelling once wrote that "the history of the world is the judgment of the world." Is this statement correct? Can the Vietnam War be interpreted as God's judgment upon the American people?

35 What Will Heaven Be Like?

Q. *Does II Peter 3:13b ("a new earth") refer to heaven?*

A. Yes, it does.

In the early part of this chapter, Peter deals with scoffers who ridicule a second coming of Christ. They do so on the basis of the fact that apparently history runs its uninterrupted course year after year and century after century. The apostle insists that there is a coming judgment and a destruction of this world as we know it. He gives an historical example of the Great Flood. Even as the Pre-Noah world was destroyed by water (vs. 6), so the post-Noah world at the second coming of Christ will be destroyed by fire (vs. 7).

Destruction, however, is not the final word.

Destruction is to be followed by renovation. And it is this renovated universe, a new heavens and a new earth, that will serve as the eternal home of the redeemed. It appears from the description given that the canopy that now separates the heavens from the earth will be removed and that restored universe will be the site of heaven for the child of God.

Its major characteristic is to be *righteousness*.

It is evident that the virtue that believers receive in Christ will be characteristic of the society of the redeemed. Acceptance of Christ as Saviour and Lord means the acquisition for him of the righteousness that Christ earned for His own on the cross. It involves forgiveness of his sins, freedom from the power of sin, and eventual freedom from all sin in his life. We acquire the first two here, freedom from the guilt and from the power of sin; we acquire the last one, freedom from the presence of sin, when our redemption is completed and Christ returns. And since that is true of the individual Christian, it also must be true of the redeemed society. All imperfection, impurity, contamination, and sin will be conspicuously absent in the new Christian world.

The application that Peter appends is this: "Wherefore, beloved, seeing that ye look for these things, give diligence that ye may be found in peace, without spot and blameless in this sight" (II Peter 3:14).

Q. *Will we recognize others in heaven?*

A. Every once in a while the Scriptures emit a gleam of light with respect to the eternal destiny of the children of God. And when they do, they emphasize that the primary joy and satisfaction for the believer will be affinity for, and vision of, the glorified Savior. John affirms in his Letter that "we shall be like him; for we shall see him even as he is" (I John 3:2).

But a secondary privilege and joy will be recognition of, and introduction to, other heirs of salvation. Apparently those who knew each other here will know each other in the next world also. When David lost a son who died at birth or shortly thereafter, he was comforted in his grief by the conviction expressed in these words: "I shall go to him, but he will not return to me" (II Sam. 12:23b). And in Jesus' teachings about the afterlife and the unbridgeable chasm that separates the saved from the lost, He stated that the rich man who had pampered himself and reduced Lazarus to paupery and then found himself in Hades lifted up his eyes and recognized "Abraham afar off, and Lazarus in his bosom" (Luke 16:23).

We will be introduced to others whom we never met in this life (cf. Matt. 8:11). And what a thrill it will be to meet and converse with Enoch, Abraham, Paul, Augustine, Luther, Calvin, and all of the other saints of God!

Q. *Will children who die in infancy be resurrected as infants or as adults? If the former, will they remain at that infant stage or continue their development?*

A. It is very true that there is a paucity of knowledge on our part with respect to the specific nature and character of our heavenly home. We know the essentials. That home is eternal and the essence of its joy and glory is communion with the Savior. Suffering, sickness, and death find no place there. All the tensions, disturbances, and shadows of this life are absent in the life to come for the child of God. But we can say little more. "Jerusalem the golden, with milk and honey blest, Beneath thy contemplation, sink heart and voice oppressed; I know not, O I know not, what joys await us there, What radiancy of glory, what bliss beyond compare!"

We do know, however, and parents may draw comfort from it, that we shall join those who have gone before. As stated in the previous section when David and Bathsheba lost an infant by death, the grieving father expressed that conviction when he said, "I shall go to him, but he will not return to me" (2 Sam. 12:23b). Death always means reunion with those who have made the previous crossing, all of them constituting that "great multitude, which no man could number, out of every nation and of all tribes and peoples and tongues, standing before the throne and before the Lamb, arrayed in white robes, and palms in their hands" (Rev. 7:9).

Although any further deductions must of necessity be speculative, it would seem that heaven is not a static state but one that is characterized by endless development for the redeemed. Someone has aptly expressed it thus: Only God has *Being;* we creatures are and always will be marked by *becoming.* We will progress constantly towards ever fuller comprehension and understanding. Talents will be sharpened, artistic abilities will be further developed, intellectual progress will go on. We never arrive. New vistas of attainment constantly beckon us on. In other words, since we are finite creatures and always will be, even in the glorified state, there is something permanently pertinent in those words of Paul to the Philippian church, "Brethren, I count not myself yet to have laid hold; but one thing I do, forgetting the things which are behind, and stretching forward to the things which are before..." (Phil. 3:13).

If this line of thinking is correct, then it may also apply to the physical, and development may proceed from the point at which death interrupted it upon earth. This raises a cluster of further questions, of course. Dr. Schilder says, "Utmost light (heaven) and utter darkness (hell) — these are extremes, and we can approach only to the border of either."

Q. *Does not I Corinthians 13:12 "then shall I know fully even as also I was fully known" imply that our knowledge in heaven will be all comprehensive?*

A. God only has complete comprehension, full penetration, and complete mastery of all that can be known. Omniscience (knowing everything) is a prerogative of the Deity, and it will remain so. Only an infinite being can have infinite knowledge.

We are finite, and finiteness means limitations. We still remain finite when we enter into the eternal world. Our capacities will be much greater than they are now, to be sure. But they will never reach the infinite.

129

There is an unbridgeable gap or chasm between the finite and the infinite, between the creature and the Creator. God will always be God; and man, even though redeemed, will still be man.

That man will remain man implies constant progress also in our heavenly learning. We will never reach the point where there is no more to know. When a child comes to adulthood (cf. vs. 11) he has new insights and broader perspectives, and as an adult (that is, if he doesn't mentally calcify by immersing himself in TV and the daily tabloid) he will keep on growing intellectually until his dying day. That exercise continues in the eternal world.

Q. *Is heaven a static place for the redeemed or will progress be registered there?*

A. There is in the Scriptures no precise, detailed description of heaven. The inspired Biblical artists paint it with broad sweeps of the brush. Every once in a while they aim to give us a glimpse of what is involved and draw a contrast between this sin-cluttered life and the sinless one beyond. They do so in order to whet the appetite and to dispense the comfort and consolation that we need.

And so there is no definite answer to the question here projected.

On the basis of the nature of man and on the basis of the Biblical teaching that heaven is to be ceaseless service of God, however, it would seem that endless development of the redeemed man is a plausible position to take.

Man, made in the image of God, is a finite being. That implies not only that he has limitations and will always have them, but that he is a growing, developing being whose aim is the ideal. God, the Creator, has *Being* but man, the finite one, has *becoming*. That is not to say that man will ever attain to the infinite — he cannot — but when God made him in His image He did constitute him a creature striving for a high goal. Sin stunts that striving or directs it to unworthy ends; redemptive grace redirects it to the highest ideals and goals. No doubt Paul was speaking in Philippians 3:13 ("forgetting the things that are behind, and stretching forward to the things that are before ...") about this life, but cannot it apply also to the glorified state? If in heaven one's talents are sharpened, artistic abilities are furthered, and native gifts are heightened, all of them designed to the praise of God and to that end alone, would not this give substance and content to our ceaseless service of God? It seems that it would, and with capacities constantly enlarging, God would be glorified in the man whom He made and redeemed.

QUESTIONS

1. Peter tells us that when the end of the world comes "the elements will melt with fire" (II Peter 3:12). Is it possible that this will be effected by the atomic and hydrogen bomb? Will man destroy himself by nuclear power?

2. The "new earth" indicates that there is continuity between this life and world and the next. We are not to be given an entirely new planet for an eternal residence; this earth is going to be renovated. What elements in our present existence will be continued in the next? Trees? Flowers? Some of our present activities? Could the position be maintained that everything we have here, exempted from sin and the effects of sin, will be continued in the next world for the Christian?

3. In your estimation, is there enough emphasis given in our Christian community to the next life? On the other hand, is it possible to be so overly concerned with Christ's return and the eternal world that we fail to do our duty towards this one? Which is the greater fault, "this-worldliness" or "other-worldliness"?

4. We are told in the Scriptures that there will be no tears, no sickness, no death, and no disappointments and sorrows for the Christian in the next world. Why is so much of this description of heaven put in negative terms?

5. Isaiah predicts that "the heavens shall be rolled together as a scroll" (Isa. 34:4; see also Rev. 6:14). Are these words intended to describe what will happen when Christ returns?

6. Is Isaiah 11:6-9 and Isaiah 65:20-25 intended to give a picture of heaven? or possibly a millennium (a thousand year reign of Christ on earth)? or simply a general picture of the Kingdom of God?

7. In I Corinthians 15 the Apostle Paul gives a fourfold description of the kinds of bodies we will have after the Great Resurrection takes place. Analyze his description. Does that body have definite continuity with the ones we now have? How did Jesus' resurrection body differ from the body He had before His passion? Did His resurrected body undergo further change when He ascended into heaven?

8. We learn in Romans 8:23 that as Christians we are "waiting for our adoption." Are we now in the position of a boy who is about to be adopted into a foster home? Explain.

9. What does it mean that we have the beginning of eternal life now? (See Matt. 19:29; 25:46; Mark 10:30; John 17:3.) Is not eternal life to be equated with an endless existence? Or is the matter of time of secondary importance?

10. One of our Christian hymns, a translation of the German "Nun Danket," contains the plea; "And free us from all ills, in this world *and the next.*" Does this hymn imply that there will be ills in the next world?

11. Jehovah's Witnesses claim, on the basis of Revelation 7:4 and 14:1, that an elite group comprising 144,000 will reside in heaven in the new world while the rest of the believers will reside here on the new earth. How do you read these passages? Is the number *144,000* to be taken literally? Or figuratively, since it is 12 times 12 taken a

thousand times? What significance do such numbers as *three, four, seven, ten,* and *twelve* have in the Book of Revelation?

12. Why is heaven compared to Mount Zion in the Scriptures?

13. Comment on this quotation from Spicer: "The positive teaching of Holy Scripture is that sin and the sinner will be blotted out of existence. There will be a clean universe again when the great controversy between Christ and Satan will be ended."

36 Is Hell a Physical State?

Q. *Is hell a physical state or simply a state of spiritual separation from God?*

A. With respect to the final state of the lost, the Bible has this to say:

1. It speaks in terms of hell as a definite place and not merely a condition. Such local designations as "prison" (I Peter 3:19), "abyss" (Luke 8:31), "furnace of fire" (Matt. 13:42), and "lake of fire" (Rev. 20:14), as well as the parable of the Rich Man and Lazarus in Luke 16 point in that direction.

2. It speaks in terms of physical as well as mental and spiritual suffering. In hell there is more than pangs of remorse (Luke 16:23, 28); there is "gnashing of teeth" (Matt. 8:12). This implies excruciating physical pain. Mark refers to it as the "unquenchable fire" (9:43) and adds that for those who suffer there, "their worm dieth not" (9:48). That latter passage is not easy to explain, but it does look in the direction of a physical torment in which the body is wracked but not consumed.

3. It speaks in terms of unending punishment for those who reject Christ. As one author says, "In Matthew 25:46 the same word describes the duration of both the bliss of the saints and the penalty of the wicked. If the latter is not, properly speaking, unending, neither is the former." Consistency would demand that if you

insist on the first, you must also concede the second. Certainly the destiny of the unbeliever is terrible to contemplate.

QUESTIONS

1. Do you think that the reality of hell is the *main* teaching of the parable of the Rich Man and Lazarus (Luke 16)? Or is that a secondary teaching? Some claim that its key is to be found in verse 29 since it was directed against the Pharisees and they, said Jesus, "set aside the Word of God by their traditions." What do you think?

2. How would you answer a man who claims that hell is really the unbroken dominion of sin, the pangs of conscience, and a feeling of despair?

3. Will lost men, who will suffer in both body and soul, suffer more than lost angels, who have no body?

4. What do you think of the following arguments, either in denial of hell or in affirming a hell of limited duration?

a. "Since man is a finite or limited creature, his sin must also be finite and therefore the punishment for it will not be endless but limited in time."

b. "If few are saved and many lost, the Devil would be victorious. But Christ came to overthrow the works of the Devil."

c. "Both Romans 5:18 and I Corinthians 15:22 teach that Christ died for all men. If He did die for all men, all men will be saved. If not, there is some imperfection in the work of Christ."

d. "God is too good to damn man eternally." Cf. also Rutherford: "Eternal torture is devoid of the property of love. A Creator that would torture his creatures eternally, would be a fiend, not a God of love."

5. Comment on these quotations:

a. From an early universalist, Charles Chauncy: "You expect to look down from heaven upon numbers of wretched objects, confined in the pit of hell, and blaspheming their creator forever. I hope to see the prison doors opened, and to hear those tongues that are now profaning the name of God, chanting his praise. In a word, you imagine that the divine glory will be advanced by immortalizing sin and misery; I by exterminating both natural and moral evil, and introducing universal happiness. Which of our systems is best supported let reason and Scripture determine."

b. From a contemporary universalist, Jitsua Marikawa: "God has already won a mighty redemption not only for us but for the entire world. . . . The redemption of the world is not dependent upon the souls we win to Jesus Christ. . . . The joyous urgency of the apostles could hardly have been rooted in the fear of damnation of all men who do not hear the gospel and accept Jesus Christ but rather in the fact that God has already reached out and made the whole human family His own. The task of the church is to tell all men that they are already God's family; that they already belong to Christ. . . . Men are no longer lost in a hell of alienation but already are in the Kingdom of fellowship and love."

Q. *What and where is Hades, to which reference is made in Revelation 1:18?*

A. The term *Hades,* which is the equivalent of the Old Testament term *Sheol,* is hard to pin down in the New Testament. It is something of a slippery term.

It has various meanings. At times it means the abode of the dead (which is not the same as the abode of departed spirits); at other times it refers to the state of death (so for instance in Acts 2:27, 31 where Peter applies it to Christ); and at times it is the equivalent of torment and punishment.

It would appear that when the word is used in connection with the righteous it is used in an *abstract* way. That is to say it does not intend to pinpoint a clearly defined, explicit geographical place where someone is imprisoned or held captive for a greater or shorter length of time.

Sometimes the term *Hades* is indicative of one of the enemies of Christ. So, for instance, in Revelation 20:14 where both Death and Hades (which are frequently found together) are personified and pictured as defeated by the Great Conqueror and thrown into the lake of fire. It seems that we have that kind of usage in Revelation 1:18. Christ is the Living One. That is, He is the Sovereign over life and death. His resurrection proves it. And by His sovereign and gracious power He conquers the dread enemies of death and the grave and rescues His people. He holds the keys. That is, He unlocks the gates of these dire consequences of sin and sets His people free.

When the term is employed in connection with the wicked, it is used figuratively and at times it has a local connotation.

In Matthew 11:23 the Lord rebukes Capernaum and predicts that it shall be brought down to Hades. It (Capernaum) had occupied a position of high privilege. It had received benefits that had been denied to others. But it had failed to make proper use of its signal blessings. For that negligence it would be deeply humiliated. That is the equivalent of going down to Hades.

In the parable of Lazarus and Dives in Luke 16 there is a *local* usage of the word. The rich man is a resident of Hades. He had failed in his religious and social responsibility, and now he was reaping his reward. Hades, the opposite of Abraham's bosom, is a place of torment and suffering. It is not the equivalent of Purgatory. Purgatory, in Roman Catholic doctrine, is a temporary state of purification. It has only one exit, and that is heaven.

Not so this place of suffering in the parable. There is an unchangeability and permanence associated with it. As such it is emblematic of hell. Sometimes it is translated in that way. Actually, however, the New Testament term for the place of eternal torment that is reserved for all who die in their sins is *Gehenna*. (Matt. 5:22, 29, 30; 10:28; 18:9; 23:15, 33; Mark 9:43; Luke 12:5; James 3:6). Hades is then a prototype of eternal woe when it is used in connection with the wicked and their destiny.

Questions

1. Why does the Bible speak of descending and going

down into Hades (Deut. 32:22; Job 11:7-9) while claiming that the spirit of man goes upward (Gen. 5:24; Ps. 16:11)?

2. What did Jesus mean by saying of His church that "the gates of Hades will not prevail against it" (Matt. 16:18)?

3. Is Psalm 16:10 ("Thou wilt not leave my soul in Hades") a prediction of Christ? If so, what does it mean?

4. Is the Beast of Revelation 13:11 whose number is 666 related in some way to Hades?

5. Is Satan a defeated enemy (John 12:31; Rev. 20:2-3, 10)? If so, how is that truth to be squared with the teaching that Satan is the prince of this world (Eph. 2:2)?

6. What is the nature of the final warning in the Book of Revelation (22:18-19)? Do these words of warning have reference simply to the Book of Revelation, or to the entire Bible? How has that prohibition been violated?

38 Is There Biblical Support for a Purgatory?

Q. Are there Biblical passages that support the doctrine of a purgatory?

A. There are three main Biblical arguments advanced, in order to prove the existence of a purgatory. Incidentally, there are extra-biblical arguments advanced also (from Tertullian, Cyril, etc.), but they date from the time when deviations from the purity of the faith had already set in. We take up these three main Biblical prooftexts in turn.

The first is I Corinthians 3:13-14 where the apostle says that "each man's work shall be made manifest: for the day shall declare it, because it is revealed in fire; and the fire itself shall prove each man's work of what sort it is." The Roman Catholics assume that this fire refers to the flames of purgatory.

Let us examine the context. There Paul is talking about ministers of the gospel. First he uses the figure of food and compares the doctrines and teachings to milk and meat (vs. 2). Then he changes the figure and uses the metaphor of planting and irrigating (vss. 6-7).

Now he uses still another metaphor. It is that of a building with its foundation and superstructure. The foundation is all-important. Jesus Christ, the atoning Son of God, is the only solid foundation. Teachers and preachers can build on that foundation "gold, silver, costly stones," that is, doctrines true to the genius of the Word of God; or "wood, hay, stubble," that is, doctrines in which there is an intermixture of human speculation. The latter will be stripped away on the Judgment Day, even as fire tests and burns away the dross. This is the loss that will be suffered (vs. 15); and if the minister retains the sure foundation, though deviating in some points and despite the faultiness in his preaching, "he himself shall be saved; yet so as through fire" (vs. 15). As is obvious, the apostle is speaking about the ministry of the gospel (he is not speaking about men in general), and as Robertson and Plummer maintain, there is not "the remotest reference to the state of the soul between death and judgment."

The second prooftext advanced by the Catholics is II Timothy 1:16-18 where Paul writes, "The Lord grant unto him to find mercy of the Lord in that day." Onesiphorus lived in Ephesus and had aided Paul in his ministry there. It is assumed that at the time of this writing he was dead and that this is Paul's prayer for his departed soul.

But this is mere assumption. Onesiphorus might still have been living. There is no hint or intimation of his death. Furthermore, these words are not really a prayer. They can well be interpreted to be no more than an expression of hope.

The third prooftext used is Revelation 21:27 where John writes about heaven, "And there shall in no wise enter into it anything unclean." It is assumed that, when a Christian dies, some uncleanness still attaches itself to him, and this impurity must be removed in purgatory before he may enter the portals of heaven. The text says no more, however, than that all impurity will be alien to heaven. And there is no shred of Biblical evidence that when a Christian dies some impurity of sin still cleaves to him. If that were commonly true, it would certainly be true of the thief who was converted on the cross. He had no opportunity at all to make amends for a bad life. But to him our Lord said, *"Today* shalt thou be with me in Paradise." No further purging is necessary for a man who dies in Christ. Salvation is complete. Christ saves "to the uttermost" (Heb. 7:25).

QUESTIONS

1. What are the Apocryphal books? Why do you find them in the Roman Catholic Bible and why do the Protestants reject them from the canon?

2. The Council of Trent stated: "If any one say that *after* the grace of justification is received the fault is so pardoned to every penitent sinner, and the guilt of temporal punishment is so blotted out that there remains no guilt of temporal punishment to be done away in this world, or that which is to come, in purgatory, before the passage can be opened into heaven, let him be accursed." Is this distinction between eternal punishment, which Christ suffered for us, and temporal punishment, which we must suffer, a Biblical one?

3. In Roman Catholic thought, one can only leave purgatory to go to heaven. How can a Christian's stay in purgatory be shortened, according to their view? And who determines when one has suffered adequate purgatorial punishment?

4. What is the relation in Roman Catholicism between purgatory and penance and indulgences?

5. It is claimed by Roman Catholicism that a Christian after death must be "ripened for glory" and "made fit for the divine presence." Does that agree with such Biblical passages as Luke 23:43; II Corinthians 5:8; Philippians 1:23; and I John 1:7?

6. A logical basis is also claimed for the purgatory doctrine. Comment on this quotation from *Our Sunday Visitor*: "Purgatory is a reality because few men, we fear, are so immaculate at death that they can stride at once into the

all-pure presence of God; and few men, we hope, are so unrepentantly depraved that they must be flung into an eternal hell." The author continues: "But are our sins not taken away by a sincere confession? In confession the mercy of God forgives our guilt, and guarantees for those sins no eternal damnation. But the majesty of God still demands satisfaction for the insult offered by these sins. It is somewhat like the case of someone sideswiping your parked car. The offender is all apology. He says: I was daydreaming. It was stupid on my part. Please forgive me. And you might tartly say: I forgive you alright, but you still have to pay for the ruined fender. Just so, in confession, God's mercy pardons but His majesty insists on reparation."

7. Amid the grief and sadness, there is an undercurrent of joy and victory on the occasion of the funeral of a Protestant Christian. This is lacking in a Roman Catholic funeral. Why is this the case?

8. In Roman Catholic thought the only Christians who do not have to spend time in purgatory are the *saints*. But, on the basis of Romans 1:7; I Corinthians 1:2; II Corinthians 1:1; Ephesians 1:1; and Colossians 1:2, who are saints in the Biblical sense of the word? How did the term undergo a change in meaning?